GO GRAMMAR! 1

A HOMEWORK AND IN-CLASS WORKBOOK

EDITION 4

A COLLINS · M COLLINS

Go Grammar! 1
4th Edition
Adrian Collins
Mark Collins

Publishing editor: Michael Spurr
Project editor: Mandy Herbet
Editor: Carolyn Glascodine
Proofreader: Sarah Blood
Permissions researcher: Debbie Gallagher
Cover design: Leigh Ashforth, Watershed Design
Text design: Leigh Ashforth, Watershed Design
Cover image: Portrait of Daniel Radcliffe by Paul Don Smith. Alamy Stock Photo/Urban Art
Production controller: Erin Dowling
Typeset by: SPi Global

Any URLs contained in this publication were checked for currency during the production process. Note, however, that the publisher cannot vouch for the ongoing currency of URLs.

For product information and technology assistance,
in Australia call **1300 790 853**;
in New Zealand call **0800 449 725**

For permission to use material from this text or product, please email
aust.permissions@cengage.com

ISBN 978 0 17 038950 1

Cengage Learning Australia
Level 7, 80 Dorcas Street
South Melbourne, Victoria Australia 3205

Cengage Learning New Zealand
Unit 4B Rosedale Office Park
331 Rosedale Road, Albany, North Shore 0632, NZ

For learning solutions, visit **cengage.com.au**

Printed in Malaysia by Papercraft.
7 8 9 25

CONTENTS

Introduction v
Author acknowledgements vi

Parts of speech

1 Concrete nouns 1
2 Abstract nouns 3
REVISION TEST 1 5
3 Action verbs 7
4 Verbs of being, sensing and relating 9
5 Verb groups 11
6 Modal verbs 13
7 Phrasal verbs 15
8 Active and passive voice 17
9 Subject and object 19
10 Subject–verb agreement 21
REVISION TEST 2 23
SPELLING FOCUS 1 25
11 Personal pronouns 29
12 Adjectives 31
13 Adjectives: comparatives and superlatives 33
14 Adverbs 35
REVISION TEST 3 37
15 Prepositions 39
16 Determiners 41
17 Phrases 43
18 Clauses 45
19 Coordinating conjunctions 47
20 Subordinating conjunctions 49
REVISION TEST 4 51

Phrases, clauses and sentences

21 Embedded clauses 53
22 Sentences (1) 55
23 Sentences (2) 57
REVISION TEST 5 59
SPELLING FOCUS 2 61

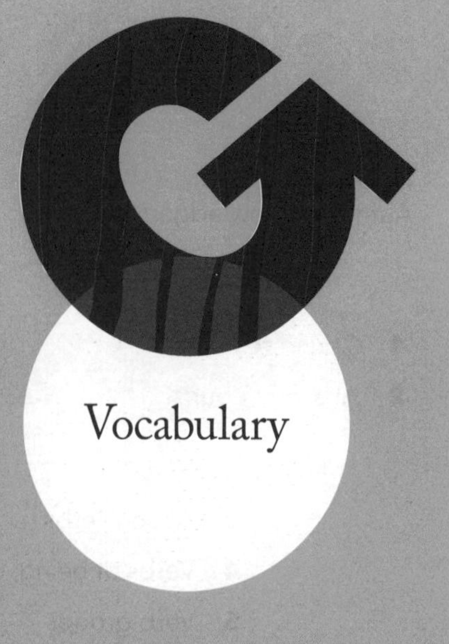

24 Prefixes and suffixes 65
25 Negative prefixes 67
26 More suffixes 69
27 Synonyms and antonyms 71
28 Inclusive language 73
29 Modality 75
30 Changes in the English language over time 77
REVISION TEST 6 79

31 Punctuating sentence endings 81
32 Commas 83
33 Apostrophes for contractions 85
34 Apostrophes for possession 87
35 Colons and semicolons 89
36 Punctuating titles 91
37 Punctuating direct speech 93
REVISION TEST 7 95
SPELLING FOCUS 3 97

38 Paragraphs and topic sentences 101
39 Cohesive ties within paragraphs 103
40 Cohesive ties across paragraphs 105
REVISION TEST 8 107

INTRODUCTION

The *Go Grammar!* series focuses on the language conventions of English: its grammar, spelling, punctuation, vocabulary and usage. This book uses the metalanguage of English – technical words such as 'preposition', 'clause', 'simile' and 'suffix' – that you need to know in order to discuss the way language is used in your writing, reading and viewing, and your speaking and listening.

This edition of *Go Grammar!* includes the terms and concepts that are covered in the Australian Curriculum: English.

Some concepts and exercises in this book will be familiar to you. You will be able to work through some sections quickly, revising material that you have already encountered. Other sections will be new to you, and you need to be quite sure that you understand each new concept before moving on to the next unit. Ask your teacher to provide exercises for extra practice if you think you need them.

Mastering these units of work will make you a better writer, reader, viewer, speaker and listener. It will also assist you in facing tests, such as NAPLAN, with more confidence.

Each unit is organised into three sections:

EXPLANATION: You will find this box at the beginning of each unit. Sometimes there is a second explanation box later in the unit, to teach you another part of the topic. Memorise these sections.

HAVE A GO: These exercises allow you to practise what you have read and memorised in the explanation. For example, you might need to show that you can identify a part of speech or that you can correctly punctuate a sentence.

TAKE IT FURTHER: These exercises are usually more challenging, allowing you to check that you really understand the topic.

You will also find in this book:

REVISION TESTS: Use these tests to make sure that you have understood the work you have done in the preceding units.

SPELLING FOCUS sections: Use these exercises to consolidate your knowledge of English spelling.

Answers to all the exercises in this book are available for your teacher. When there is more than one possible response, we suggest that you work with a partner to check each other's answers. Working with a partner is a good way of making sure that you have understood every topic.

We hope you enjoy working through the exercises in this book and discover new and interesting things about grammar.

AUTHOR ACKNOWLEDGEMENTS

To my children and parents for their kindly light. To Mark, my big brother writer, thank you for your always considerate collaboration.

Adrian Collins

To my family and parents, who see the wood from the trees. To my co-author brother, Adrian, thank you for your good-humoured sense and sensibility.

Mark Collins

Name:	Due date:	Guardian signature:

1 CONCRETE NOUNS

Parts of speech

Nouns belong to two broad groups: concrete nouns and abstract nouns. Concrete nouns include:

→ common nouns, such as *woman, lion* and *table*
→ proper nouns, such as *Brisbane* and *Judith Wright*
→ and collective nouns, such as *team, choir, convoy* and *mob*.

For a quick way to check whether a word can be used as a noun, try adding it to the gaps in one of these sentences. Does it fit?

e.g. (The) ________ is good. For example: The *food* is good. *Food* is plentiful in Australia.
(The) ________ are good. For example: *Chinese stir-fries* are good. *Chinese stir-fries* were delicious. *Chinese stir-fries* are a family favourite.

The definite article *the* is used sometimes, but not always, before a noun, as is the indefinite article (*a* or *an*). Determiners *some* and *any* and numbers can also fit before the noun.

HAVE A GO

1 In the following school bulletin, circle eight common nouns, underline three proper nouns and tick four collective nouns. Remember to check if the word fits the gaps in the sentences above.

Sporting teams participating in the carnival at Ballarat next Friday will leave the school at recess in a fleet of buses. The choir and the orchestra will also be going, as they have been chosen to perform the national anthem. Notes and money must be handed in to the office by Wednesday.

2 Write the correct proper noun in each column. Check your school atlas or search online to find the correct capital city and country in the Asia–Pacific region.

	Country	Capital city
a	Australia	
b		Suva
c		Jakarta
d	Malaysia	
e	Papua New Guinea	
f		Wellington
g		Manila
h	Singapore	
i	Solomon Islands	
j	Vanuatu	

Capital letters are needed for proper nouns such as *Melbourne*, *Lydia* and the *Sydney Opera House*.

European settlers applied conventional, collective nouns to groups of animals they encountered in a strange, new land called Australia. For instance, a *mob* is a collective noun used for kangaroos but some Indigenous people use *mob* to describe themselves.

3 Draw lines to match the common nouns with the most appropriate collective nouns. Check your dictionary if you are unfamiliar with any of these collective nouns.

	Common nouns	Collective nouns
a	taxis	team
b	kangaroos	swarm
c	singers	flock
d	footballers	convoy
e	fish	bouquet
f	flowers	choir
g	trucks	fleet
h	bees	mob
i	sheep	shoal

TAKE IT FURTHER

1 Look up an Australian idiom each week.

In your notebook, record a word (or expression) you have heard that you don't know its meaning. Ask your teacher to set up an alert for a class 'digital word a week' activity: each week a student sends the word of the week to the teacher who alerts all members of the class. This exercise could build your knowledge of Australian idiom and slang and their appropriate cultural context.

For example, 'horse's doovers' means ____. (write in the meaning)

2 Write the appropriate collective noun to match the common noun in the following student exercise to remember tricky collective nouns.

It's like playing with a pack of cards when I try to remember collective nouns. When I look into the sea near a pier, I see a shoal/school of fish and near to the horizon a pod/herd/school of dolphins but when I look down at my feet an army of ants moves faster than a herd of elephants on the run from a swarm/bike/drift/hive of bees, a clowder of feral cats, a band of gorillas and a troop of monkeys. It's quite confusing thinking about collective nouns for animals. Some choices for collective nouns sound strange to me but I enjoy a visit to the RSPCA kennels to see a litter of pups. It's a pleasant change from a crowd of noisy marchers in the city.

Name:	Due date:	Guardian signature:

2 ABSTRACT NOUNS

Parts of speech

An **abstract noun** is a word for naming an idea, concept, quality, event or feeling.

e.g. Sometimes my *mood* swings from *excitement* and *happiness* to *disappointment* and *sadness*. *History* is often about the *struggle* for *freedom* and *equality*.

Remember that an abstract noun is intangible. You cannot apply the five senses to an idea; you cannot touch or hold or interact with a concept, such as democracy, courage and truth. An abstract noun is the opposite of a concrete noun (which is tangible), such as pizza, book and beach.

1 Write the nouns below in the correct column of the table.

kindness	dream	netball	herd
thought	tablet	arrogance	Dian Fossey
truth	concern	cottage	Elizabeth Blackburn
pleasure	container	honour	humility
schoolbag	vegetable	courage	wheelbarrow
glass	child	pride	excitement

Concrete nouns	Abstract nouns
Example: child	**Example:** concern

2 Have you heard of Mr Darcy? *Pride and Prejudice* (1813), by Jane Austen, is a delightful comedy of manners and the novel has much to say about 'property', money, status and judgement in choosing a suitable marriage partner.

a Read Austen's clever introduction (the first two paragraphs) to her popular novel on the next page and underline the abstract nouns. How many abstract nouns are there in total? ____

To become a better writer, build your vocabulary of abstract nouns.

> It is a truth universally acknowledged, that a single man in possession of a good fortune, must be in want of a wife.
>
> However little known the feelings or views of such a man may be on his first entering a neighbourhood, this truth is so well fixed in the minds of the surrounding families, that he is considered the rightful property of some one or other of their daughters.
>
> Austen, J 1813, *Pride and Prejudice*.

b What does it mean when someone shows 'pride' but another person expresses 'prejudice'? Consult a dictionary but work out your own meaning from your experience. You can refer to a film or book you are studying in class for examples. Write your response in two short sentences, one explaining what *pride* means and the second explaining what *prejudice* means. Give an example of each.

3 In the word families below, circle the abstract noun.

- **a** amusement, amuse, amusing, amusingly
- **b** embolden, boldness, bold, boldly
- **c** courageous, encourage, courage, courageously
- **d** disappointedly, disappoint, disappointed, disappointment
- **e** encourage, encouragement, encouraging, encouragingly
- **f** excitably, excite, excitable, excitement
- **g** glorious, glorify, glory, gloriously
- **h** grieve, grief, grievous, grievously
- **i** joyful, enjoy, joy, joyfully
- **j** obedience, obey, obedient, obediently

Abstract nouns are useful when you are creating your own texts, particularly when you are putting forward your view of films, books and media.

Read this excerpt from a student's book poster promoting *Of Mice and Men* (1937) by John Steinbeck. Fill in the blank letters below to complete these abstract nouns, which are useful in literary discussion and analysis.

> Most characters suffer from lone_____ess and lack of imag_____tion to make their own dest____y. Lennie has the intel________ce of a child and cannot deal with his f___r of Curley who tries to show his mascu_____ity by bullying others rather than showing ki___ness. Steinbeck shows sym_____hy for kind characters like Lennie and cont____pt for cruel characters like Curley.

Name: Due date: Guardian signature:

Parts of speech

REVISION TEST 1

1 In the sentences below, some words are used more than once, as both common and proper nouns. All proper nouns need a capital letter. Rewrite the sentences with the necessary capital letters.

a The australian national university, the university of melbourne and the university of sydney are among the top-ranking universities in australia.

______

______

b When angela goes to church at easter and christmas, she likes to admire the gothic architecture and stained glass windows in st mary's church.

______

______

c ahmed and fatima gave an informative talk about their muslim faith and the mosques of turkey, focusing on the blue mosque.

______

______

d One of australia's most remarkable natural gifts, the great barrier reef, is the largest reef in the world.

______

______

e As well as being the name of a city, new york is one of the states in the united states of america.

______

______

2 Here are 10 abstract nouns and common nouns taken from a discussion of audience appeal in films. Write them in the correct column of the table.

humour	theme	lighting	camera	engagement
music	costume	make-up	sensitivity	tragedy

Abstract nouns	Common nouns

3 Add the missing abstract noun to each word family below.

	Noun	Verb	Adjective	Adverb
a		amuse	amusing	amusingly
b		embolden	bold	boldly
c		encourage	courageous	courageously
d		disappoint	disappointed	disappointedly
e		glorify	glorious	gloriously
f		enjoy	joyful	joyfully
g		obey	obedient	obediently
h		pacify	peaceful	peacefully
i		terrify	terrible	terribly
j		weaken	weak	weakly

4 Underline the 11 abstract nouns in this character profile from a student ensemble script.

Mia's young love for Ethan shows persistence and blindness. She pursues her lover in secrecy and with haste. She does not tell her parents that she texts him day and night, forgets to hand in her homework and, combined with events beyond her control, turns to digital distraction until her best friend tells her, 'I hope that drip isn't still after you. You deserve better!'

5 The extract below is the famous opening to *A Tale of Two Cities* (1859) by Charles Dickens. Complete the abstract nouns by adding the blank letters.

It was the best of times, it was the worst of times, it was the age of wis___m, it was the age of fool_____ness, it was the epoch of bel____f, it was the epoch of incred______ty, it was the season of Lig__t, it was the season of Dark_____s, it was the spring of h__pe, it was the winter of d____pair, we had everything before us, we had nothing before us, we were all going direct to Hea____n, we were all going direct the other way—in short, the period was so far like the present period, that some of its noisiest authorities insisted on its being received, for g____d or for ev___l, in the superlative degree of compa____son only.

Dickens, C 1859, *A Tale of Two Cities*.

6 Many nouns have unusual plural forms. Write the plural of each word in the right-hand column, taking care to spell it correctly.

	Word	Plural
a	ally	
b	army	
c	brush	
d	child	
e	church	

	Word	Plural
f	family	
g	goose	
h	hero	
i	knife	
j	tooth	

Name:	Due date:	Guardian signature:

3 ACTION VERBS

Parts of speech

An **action verb** is usually an action or doing word. Most, but not all, verbs are action verbs.

 Rocco *remembered* the school policy on cyber bullying.
Maria *changed* her mobile plan.

Here is a quick way to check whether a word can be used as a verb: try adding the infinitive form of the verb (for example to *run*, to *see*, minus to) in the gap in the sentence below.

e.g. They can ______. For example: They can *run*.

1 Underline the action verbs in the following sentences.

- **a** Theo and Jackie won the writing competition.
- **b** They lost the preliminary final.
- **c** Nina cancelled her holiday to Bali.
- **d** They built stylish homes.
- **e** Some junior students participated in the fun run.
- **f** I received a certificate in the Premier's Reading Competition.
- **g** She painted our house.
- **h** Federal and state elections require much money and planning.
- **i** Maria awoke in the night from a strange dream.
- **j** Students rushed to the canteen for a special treat of strawberries and yoghurt.

2 Complete the word families table by writing action verbs in the verb column. Remember that you can check whether a word is a verb if it will fit in the gap in this sentence: They can ______.

	Noun	Verb	Adjective	Adverb
a	enjoyment		enjoyable	enjoyably
b	hurry		hurried	hurriedly
c	laughter		laughable	laughably
d	mourning		mournful	mournfully
e	persuasion		persuasive	persuasively
f	rebel		rebellious	rebelliously
g	striker		striking	strikingly
h	terror		terrible	terribly
i	information		informative	informatively
j	sadness		sad	sadly

Most, but not all, verbs are 'doing' words or action verbs.

TAKE IT FURTHER

1 Underline the nine action verbs that emphasise collaborative learning.

- **a** We connect through stories we share.
- **b** We picture our lives in images.
- **c** We keep and share knowledge through art, drama and music.
- **d** We work with others to celebrate our understanding of our world.
- **e** We discuss different ideas together and build our knowledge.

2 To improve your writing, choose strong, precise action verbs. Choose from the box below the best synonym for the verb *walk* in each of the following sentences.

dawdled	marched	stalked	strutted	toddled
shuffled	filed	strolled	tramped	trekked

- **a** The soldiers *walked* quickly. ____________________
- **b** The models *walked* along the runway. ____________________
- **c** The boys *walked* to school. ____________________
- **d** The hikers *walked* through the bush. ____________________
- **e** Tourists *walked* along the promenade. ____________________
- **f** The old man *walked* to his chair. ____________________
- **g** The baby *walked* to her mother. ____________________
- **h** The scouts *walked* the Kokoda Trail. ____________________
- **i** The students *walked* out of assembly in orderly lines. ____________________

3 Many words can be used as either nouns or verbs. In the pairs of sentences below, underline the italicised word when it is used as a verb.

- **a** i I went to a *play* last night.
  - ii He is going to *play* in the garden.
- **b** i I like to go for a *run* after school.
  - ii I *run* around the oval most afternoons.
- **c** i I will *change* trains at Flinders Street.
  - ii I'm going to transfer to a different sport next term; I'd like a *change*.
- **d** i Stand in the *centre* of the circle.
  - ii Our program will *centre* on strategies for keeping fit.
- **e** i I *hope* you will like this book.
  - ii He's our best *hope* for the competition.

Name:	Due date:	Guardian signature:

4 VERBS OF BEING, SENSING AND RELATING

Parts of speech

Action verbs are also called event verbs or happening verbs. There are a few common verbs that are not about action or doing; they are about a **state**, such as being, sensing or relating. These are sometimes called linking verbs.

e.g. I *am* a student.

He *was* a teacher before he *became* an actor.

I *feel* tired.

She *seems* hungry.

He *looks* terrific.

The most common verb in English is the verb **to be**. It has its own special forms.

e.g. Canberra *is* the capital city of Australia.

Public transport *was* an issue in the state election.

Hospital services in country regions *will be* addressed in the budget.

		Singular (one)	Plural (more than one)
Present tense	**first person**	I am	we are
	second person	you are	you are
	third person	he/she/it is	they are
Past tense	**first person**	I was	we were
	second person	you were	you were
	third person	he/she/it was	they were
Future tense	**first person**	I will be	we will be
	second person	you will be	you will be
	third person	he/she/it will be	they will be

1 Underline the seven forms of *being* verbs in the following paragraph of creative writing based on an ensemble performance of William Shakespeare's play *The Tempest*.

Whoosh! It was not a normal human being but a smelly, grotty monster who said his name was Caliban and that he wanted to escape. He told me to be his god but he sounded drunk and was wobbling as he tried to shake my hand. As he came closer to me, his eyes were fierce and devilish. He shouted, 'I will be free!' I replied, 'I cannot be your god of deliverance'. Then he vanished and I awoke from my dream.

The verb *to be* is the most common of the 'state' verbs.

2 Write the appropriate tense (past, present or future) of the verb *to be* in the spaces below.

a 'I ____________ not happy,' said Mrs Carbunkle, who ____________ grumpy by nature. 'That comment earlier ____________ very naughty of you, Tom. Your mother ____________ very disappointed when she hears about it.'

b It ____________ the end of term and the students ____________ tired. 'I know that you ____________ sick of school, but tomorrow you ____________ to finish this work, or you ____________ doing it for homework during the break.'

c Sara told me she ____________ not as excited about the sequel as she ____________ about the first film. 'The first one ____________ great!' said Sara. 'I don't think this one will be ____________ any good because the same actors ____________ not in it!'

3 Underline the linking verbs in the following sentences.

a I will become an engineer.
b She is feeling quite sad.
c You look really happy this morning.
d You sound tired.
e He became one of the greatest actors of his generation.
f They seem keen about the match this afternoon.

TAKE IT FURTHER

Circle the being, sensing or relating verbs, then underline the action verbs in the extract below from *Emma* (1816) by Jane Austen.

Human nature is so well disposed towards those who are in interesting situations, that a young person, who either marries or dies, is sure of being kindly spoken of.

A week had not passed since Miss Hawkins's name was first mentioned in Highbury, before she was, by some means or other, discovered to have every recommendation of person and mind; to be handsome, elegant, highly accomplished, and perfectly amiable: and when Mr Elton himself arrived to triumph in his happy prospects, and circulate the fame of her merits, there was very little more for him to do, than to tell her Christian name, and say whose music she principally played.

Mr Elton returned, a very happy man. He had gone away rejected and mortified—disappointed in a very sanguine hope, after a series of what had appeared to him strong encouragement; and not only losing the right lady, but finding himself debased to the level of a very wrong one. He had gone away deeply offended—he came back engaged to another – and to another as superior, of course, to the first, as under such circumstances what is gained always is to what is lost.

Austen, J 1816, *Emma*.

Name: | Due date: | Guardian signature:

5 VERB GROUPS

Parts of speech

Verbs are often used in **verb groups**. Verb groups (also called compound verbs) consist of:

→ one or more auxiliary (or 'helping') verbs and a verb participle. Participles that end in *–ing* are called present participles. They express an action or state which happens at this moment. Participles that end in *–ed* are called past participles. They express an action or state which is already completed

e.g. The gardener *is working* very hard. (action happening at this moment)
The champion *has played* here many times. (completed action)

→ an auxiliary verb and the form of the verb called the infinitive (the form that has no tense, number or person).

e.g. The gardener *will work* tomorrow.
The champion *will play* here next week.

The most common auxiliary verbs are:

→ *have, has, had* (followed by a past participle)

→ *am, is, are, was, were* (followed by a present participle).

1 Complete the table with the missing participles. Auxiliary verbs have been included in brackets to help you.

	Present tense	Present participle	Past participle
a	talk	(is)	(has)
b	brush	(was)	(had)
c	fill	(were)	(have)
d	attend	(am)	(have)
e	look	(are)	(had)
f	perform	(was)	(has)

2 While most verbs in the past tense simply add *–ed*, some irregular verbs form their past participles differently. Complete the table with the missing irregular participles. Auxiliary verbs have been included in brackets to help you. Use your dictionary if you need further help.

	Present tense	Present participle	Past participle
a	eat	(am)	(had)
b	teach	(am)	(have)
c	sink	(am)	(have)
d	go	(is)	(has)
e	do	(was)	(has)
f	think	(am)	(had)
g	try	(are)	(have)

When writing narratives, be careful to keep your tense consistent.

Auxiliary verbs are used to form all tenses other than the simple present (*I walk*) and the simple past (*I walked*). They allow all kinds of fine distinctions: *I had been walking for hours. I walked 10 kilometres yesterday. I have been walking regularly each morning. I will be walking across the mountains on my trip.*

The verb *have* (and its forms *has* and *had*) is mostly used as an auxiliary verb.

e.g. I *have finished* my assignment.
He *had sent* me an email.

However, the verb *have* can also be used as an ordinary action verb.

e.g. I *have* a cold.
Your mother *has* your lunch in her bag.

1 Complete these sentences with the simple past form of the verb.

- **a** I ____________________ (have) a sore throat.
- **b** Parking inspectors ____________________ (patrol) the carpark twice a day.
- **c** The curators ____________________ (prepare) a good wicket for the women's Twenty20 game.
- **d** More than a thousand people ____________________ (run) in a city marathon this year.
- **e** Two construction companies ____________________ (begin) the Metro Tunnel in August.

2 Complete these sentences using an auxiliary and a participle.

- **a** Yesterday I ____________________ (do) my homework when the fire alarm went off.
- **b** At last I ____________________ (finish) all my assignments for this term.
- **c** Next weekend, we ____________________ (go) camping.
- **d** The teacher said that I ____________________ (work) really hard on my assignment before my illness.
- **e** Sam ______________________________ (brush) his teeth extra well because he is going to the dentist.
- **f** The Youngs ____________________ (live) in the same house for 30 years.
- **g** Ella ____________________ (have) that bike for so long that she ____________________ (grow) out of it.
- **h** My cousin ____________________ (arrive) home before I appeared.

3 From a grammatical point of view, the simple future tense is formed by an auxiliary (*will*) and the infinitive minus *to* (for example *walk*). But English has a number of ways of suggesting future time. Underline all the sentences below that express the future.

- **a** I am going to trek across the mountains next week.
- **b** Tomorrow I leave for Hobart.
- **c** I will call you tomorrow.
- **d** I am going to ring him in the morning.
- **e** I sent him a text.
- **f** I left for Hobart at midday.

Name: | Due date: | Guardian signature:

6 MODAL VERBS

Parts of speech

Modal verbs are auxiliary verbs that help us to express degrees of certainty, probability, possibility or obligation.

May I go to the toilet, Miss? (request)

I *can* come tomorrow. (possibility)

According to her itinerary, she *must* be in Paris now. (certainty)

I *ought* to come tomorrow. (obligation)

I *must* attend the information session tomorrow. (obligation)

Modal verbs include *can*, *could*, *must*, *would*, *shall*, *should* and *ought*.

Will can also be a modal verb. Mostly it is used for events that occur in the future, but it can also be used to express probability.

It *will* rain tomorrow. (future)

It *might* rain. (possibility)

It looks like it *will* rain soon. (probability)

I *will* get my way, whatever you say! (certainty)

1 Underline the modal verbs in the following sentences.

- **a** May I offer you an entrée or a pre-dinner drink, Sir?
- **b** My English report says I must improve my vocabulary and sentence structure.
- **c** You must see this movie about bridesmaids and cops.
- **d** She might have forgotten to apply for a visa.
- **e** We could do more to help the needy.
- **f** If you help to improve my serve, I just might be able to win the tennis match.
- **g** I told my little brother he must only cross when he sees the green walk sign.
- **h** They can work well when they put their minds to the task.

2 Modal verbs are used to suggest particular shades of meaning. Write *obligation*, *request*, *possibility* or *probability* after each of the following sentences to indicate which one fits with the meaning.

- **a** We *must* all do our bit to recycle batteries and globes. ______________________
- **b** It *could* have been a disaster. ______________________
- **c** *May* I leave early for my music lesson, please, Miss? ______________________
- **d** I *ought* to start my homework before dinner. ______________________
- **e** *Would* you like to open the window? ______________________
- **f** I am sure that she *will* be here tomorrow. ______________________
- **g** She *may* come tomorrow. ______________________
- **h** All mobile phones *must* be left at home. ______________________

Modal verbs can be used to express subtle shades of meaning.

3 Modal verbs can suggest different degrees of intensity. In each of the groups below, rank the sentences from *most* to *medium* to *least intense.*

a i You *must* do your homework. ____________

ii You *could* do your homework. ____________

iii You *should* do your homework. ____________

b i I *may* conquer the world. ____________

ii I *will* conquer the world. ____________

iii I *can* conquer the world. ____________

c i She *may* have taken the money. ____________

ii She *must* have taken the money. ____________

iii She *could* have taken the money. ____________

d i I was worried when you were late; you *could* have rung me. ____________

ii I was worried when you were late; you *should* have rung me. ____________

iii I was worried when you were late; *would* you ring me next time? ____________

e i We *shall* overcome! ____________

ii We *could* overcome. ____________

iii *Might* we overcome? ____________

TAKE IT FURTHER

1 Underline the eight modal verbs in the following brief reflection on comics at a writer's festival.

You might like to call comics visual narratives or graphic novels. The latter term could be a catchword but if it gets people reading then it could fire a young person's imagination. Comics could or should be satirical. They might look easy to create, but one illustrator took more than 20 hours to produce each page of his comic book, while the adolescent reader might have taken only a minute to read it. Would you put that kind of effort into making art for young readers?

2 Your choice of modal verbs is very important when you want to persuade someone of something. People usually don't like to be given orders with an offensive or off-putting choice of words. Work with a partner to decide which sentence in each of the following pairs is more effective. Tick the boxes after the sentences you think are more effective.

a i I *can't* submit my homework until Monday, Sir. ☐

ii *Could* I please submit my homework on Monday, Sir? ☐

b i Customers paying with credit cards *must* use this check-out. ☐

ii Customers paying with credit cards *can* use this check-out. ☐

c i I *must* have the chicken; I don't eat fish. ☐

ii I *would* like to have the chicken please; I don't eat fish. ☐

d i *Would* you follow me, please, Madam? ☐

ii You *must* follow me, Madam. ☐

Name:	Due date:	Guardian signature:

7 PHRASAL VERBS

Parts of speech

Many verbs in English are made up of a main word followed by one or more short words. The short words are words that can be used as prepositions (see Unit 15) or adverbs (see Unit 14), but they do not behave like prepositions or adverbs. The connection between the words can be puzzling for people learning English. These verbs are called **phrasal verbs** or multiword verbs and they are one of the fastest-growing features of modern colloquial English.

I won't *put up with* that noise any longer.

He says that he won't *go through with* the plan.

We need to *get up* early.

We *slowed down* when we saw the police.

The heavy rain will *slow up* the traffic.

He *cut in* when I was talking.

Your electricity will be *cut off* if you don't pay the bill.

Cut it *out*! You can't expect me to believe that!

Phrasal verb, such as *cut to the chase, a piece of cake and kick the bucket*, are often examples **idiomatic language**. You have to understand the whole expression; you can't analyse each word (*cut?*, *chase?*) in order to determine the meaning. Similarly, there is no logic to the fact that the phrasal verbs *slow up* and *slow down* have the same meaning.

Phrasal verbs are particularly common in speech and may be inappropriate in formal writing. They can often be replaced by a one-word verb, which is usually a much longer verb with several syllables. Perhaps one reason why we use so many phrasal verbs in English is that they are easier to use in everyday speech and writing.

1 Choose from the box a one-word verb to replace the phrasal verb in italics in each sentence. Note that the parts of the phrasal verb may be separated.

confessed	failed	eroded	force
decelerated	consume	supervise	accommodate
tolerate	manage	extinguish	avoiding

a We *slowed down* when we saw the police. ____________

b Will you *look after* the children? ____________

c I don't know how he manages to *put away* so much food. ____________

d My brother is always looking for a way of *getting out of* the housework. ____________

e You must *put out* the fire. ____________

f How are we going to *deal with* this problem? ____________

g Part of the cliff *broke away* after the storm. ____________

h I won't *put up with* that any longer. ____________

i Could you *put* me *up* for a week while my house is being painted? ____________

j The offender *owned up* to his crime. ____________

k I *stuffed up* my test. ____________

l You will need to *break down* the door. ____________

Phrasal verbs are more appropriate in colloquial language than formal writing.

2 Add the missing words to complete the phrasal or multiword verbs in the following informal sentences. Some sentences may need more than one word.

a I speed ______________ once I pass the school.

b You would be wise to hand ______________ your assignment on time.

c He is planning to take ______________ sailing.

d I need to take ______________ the waistband as I've lost so much weight.

e I can't make ______________ the handwriting.

f We need to make ______________ the whole room.

g Are you telling me you made ______________ that story?

h Don't bring ______________ these problems at the meeting.

i The plane will take ______________ at eight o'clock.

j I'm sorry for the interruption but please now move ______________ the task.

k I have tried to like his brother, but I just don't get ______________ him.

l I'm warning you now that you won't ______________ with this!

TAKE IT FURTHER

1 Complete the phrasal verbs in the following catchy advertisement for an environmentally friendly caravan.

Load ______ and rev ______ with this new eco caravan. It will fire ______ retired couples who want to live ______ the land and kick ______ their shoes at night when they camp in out-of-the-way places with minimum impact on their surroundings. This beaut van is solar-powered and generator-free so it gives ______ no toxic fumes and runs ______ Aussie soy bio-fuel. You'll be over the moon!

2 One of the words most commonly used in phrasal verbs is *get* (past tense *got*): *get up, get off, get down, get with; got up, got off, got down, got with*. It is almost impossible to avoid *get* and *got* in colloquial language but try to avoid using *get* and *got* in formal written language. Rewrite the following sentences, replacing the phrasal verb containing *get* with a more formal verb.

a All staff are urged to get with the new programs.

b I cannot think of any way of getting around the problem.

c The terrorist got killed by a police sniper.

Name:	Due date:	Guardian signature:

8 ACTIVE AND PASSIVE VOICE

Parts of speech

Active voice occurs when the subject of the sentence is the doer of the action.

 *Alex* drives a car.

What is the action? The verb *drives*.

Ask *who?* or *what?* before the main verb to find the subject of the sentence.

→ Who or what drives? Alex. *Alex* is the subject.

→ Who is the doer of the action? Alex.

The subject of the sentence is the doer of the action. The sentence is in the active voice. Most sentences in English are active. Sometimes, we want to put the emphasis on the object of the action:

 The car *was driven* by Alex.

What is the action? The verb *was driven*.

Ask *who?* or *what?* before the main verb to find the subject of the sentence.

→ Who or what (was) *driven?* The car. *Car* is the subject.

However, the car is obviously not the doer of the action. The sentence is in the passive voice.

You can often recognise the passive by the structure *is/are, was/were, will be* + *(past participle)* + *by.*

 We will be chauffeured by my mother. (Who or what *chauffered*? Answer: *my mother*)

The children were encouraged by the teacher to read myths. (Who or what *encouraged*? Answer: *the teacher*)

Maths is taught by Ms Patel. (Who or what *taught*? Answer: *Ms Patel*)

1 Circle the subject and underline the verb in the following sentences.

a William Shakespeare wrote the play.

b The chef cooked the fish on the barbecue.

c The parents' association reminded the Minister of Education to spend more money on school libraries.

d Young backpackers from overseas work in some tourist hospitality services.

e The police arrested several protesters.

2 Rewrite the sentences in question 1 in the passive voice. The start of each sentence has been done for you.

a The play ______________________________

b The fish ______________________________

c The Minister of Education ______________________________

____

Use active voice unless you have a specific need for the passive.

d Some tourist hospitality services ______________________________

____

e Several protesters ______________________________

3 Underline the sentences that are in the passive voice.

a New economic priorities were announced by the government.
b The government announced new economic priorities.
c The border is patrolled by guards.
d Guards patrol the border.
e Trespassers will be prosecuted.
f The winners will be announced on Friday.
g The principal will announce the winners on Friday.
h Acid was added to the liquid.

1 Underline the use of the passive voice in this opinion piece on wolves.

Remember the children's story about the big bad wolf? I think this fearful image is shared by too many adults who use it as an excuse to hunt and kill this shy animal. It's rare that a wolf is glimpsed by a human. Wolves know that people are not to be trusted. A vital ecological role is played by the wolf. Biodiversity is maintained by wolves who remove weak and injured animals in the wild, such as deer, making herds stronger over time. The red wolf is critically endangered by loss of habitat, farming and humans hunting for pleasure.

2 Rewrite the following thank you note in the active voice. Remember to ask *who?* or *what?* before the main verb in each sentence to find the subject of the main verb.

Dear Ms Alexander

Thank you for the great experience of outdoor learning in the garden. The posters made by our class were really fun. The video footage taken by GoPro cameras and stories using tablet footage were shared by the whole class. Some new words were learnt by each student.

Toby Year 7

Dear Ms Alexander

Toby Year 7

Name:	Due date:	Guardian signature:

9 SUBJECT AND OBJECT

Parts of speech

The two most important elements of a sentence are the **subject** and the **verb**.

e.g. My mother and father cried at the funeral.
(subject: My mother and father; verb: cried)

An easy way to identify the subject is to ask *who?* or *what?* before the verb.

e.g. Ellie hit the ball for a home run.
Question: *Who* hit the ball?
Answer: Ellie.
Therefore, *Ellie* is the subject of the verb.

Many verbs also have an **object**.

e.g. The dog chased the ball.
(verb: chased; object: the ball)

An easy way to identify the object is to ask *whom?* or *what?* after the verb.

e.g. Ellie hit the ball for a home run.
Question: Ellie hit *whom?* Ellie hit *what?*
Answer: The ball.
Therefore, *the ball* is the object of the verb.

1 Some sentences just have a subject–verb (S–V) pattern. Write S for subject and V for verb above the appropriate words in the sentences below. Remember to ask *who?* or *what?* **before** the verb to find the subject.

a The dog barked.

b The cat yowled.

c The dog has been barking all night.

d The neighbour's cat yowled in sympathy.

2 Write S for subject, V for verb and O for object above the appropriate words in the sentences below. Remember to ask *who?* or *what?* **before** the verb to find the subject, and *whom?* or *what?* **after** the verb to find the object.

a The goat butted the fence.

b The elephant trampled the crops.

c A large herd of elephants has trampled the newly planted crops.

d The white goat with big horns butted the rickety fence.

e Australian gymnasts perform difficult routines in international competitions.

To find the subject of a verb, ask *who?* or *what?* before the verb.

3 Each of the sentences below has a collective noun as the subject. From each pair of sentences, underline the one in which the collective noun agrees with a plural verb.

a i The class was quietly working through the maths exercises.

ii The class were in an uproar, hurling insults at each other.

b i The audience was applauding loudly.

ii The audience were predominantly older people.

c i The team, accompanied by tired parents, arrive for training any time between six and seven.

ii The team arrives at training about seven o'clock.

d i The young couple has put down a deposit on a house.

ii The young couple were discussing which house to buy.

e i The committee has voted unanimously in favour of the proposal.

ii The committee members are selected from all the classes in the school.

4 It can be more difficult to identify the subject when it is part of a noun group or when it is followed by such phrases as *as well as*, *in addition to* or *apart from*. In the following sentences, underline the subject and then circle the form of the verb that agrees with the subject.

a A drill, in addition to a safety mask and gloves, (is / are) required for this job.
b The hem of the curtains (was / were) drenched in rainwater.
c See the rats in the laboratory (runs / run).
d The soccer player (hug / hugs) her teammates when a goal is scored.
e The soccer players (hug / hugs) their teammates when a goal is scored.
f A chorus of clapping and shouting (greet / greets) the final siren.
g The team manager with several helpers (brings / bring) out the half-time drinks.
h The trophy, in addition to a pile of certificates, (were / was) placed on the table in preparation for the ceremony.

Each, *every*, *everyone*, *everybody*, *no-one* and *nobody* require a singular verb. When singular subjects are joined by *either … or* or *neither … nor*, they also require a singular verb.

In the following sentences, underline the correct form of the verb from the choices given in brackets.

a Every school girl and boy (was / were) encouraged to attend the senior play.

b Everybody (needs / need) to bring a notebook and a pen.

c Each peach and apricot (is / are) checked for quality.

d Neither a threat nor reward (delivers / deliver) the truth.

e Neither the girl in the blue jacket nor the boy in the red vest (seems / seem) to have the visitor's guide.

REVISION TEST 2

1 Underline the action verbs in the following sentences.

- **a** Jackie won the writing competition after writing three drafts of her story.
- **b** My team lost the final but were happy with their effort.
- **c** Amad cancelled his appointment.
- **d** They built expensive homes with high fences.
- **e** Some senior students participated in the bushfire appeal.
- **f** Ten students in Year 8 received a certificate for the wider reading competition.
- **g** The presidential candidate declared her health was sound.
- **h** We planted some new trees around the school oval.
- **i** The school tuckshop banned food with high fat and sugar content.

2 Underline the verbs in the following sentences. Then write the required tense of the verb.

> *e.g.* Tara and I *swam* two kilometres during training yesterday.
> Future tense: *will swim*

- **a** The school band will sound outstanding at the concert. *Past tense*: ____________________
- **b** Dan only wrote 10 lines for his essay. *Present tense*: ____________________
- **c** I waited for you at the school gate for a good chat. *Present tense*: ____________________
- **d** I will fix my bike at the weekend. *Past tense*: ____________________
- **e** He can teach biology. *Past tense*: ____________________
- **f** I may be performing in the school play. *Future tense*: ____________________
- **g** I bought roses for my mum. *Future tense*: ____________________

3 Write the appropriate tense (*past*, *present* or *future*) of the verb *to be* in the spaces below.

- **a** 'I *will be* (______________) ready in five minutes,' she said. You know that I *am* (______________) always punctual. You *were* (______________) 10 minutes late as usual.
- **b** I told you that we *were* (______________) early. I *was* (______________) right; there *was* (______________) no need to leave until three o'clock.

4 Complete these sentences using an auxiliary and a participle.

> *e.g.* Yesterday I was doing (do) my homework when the fire alarm went off.

- **a** I ______________________________ (finish) my English assignment.
- **b** Next weekend, we ______________________________ (go) camping.
- **c** The teacher said that I ______________________________ (work) really hard on my assignment over the last two weeks.

5 Underline the phrasal verb in each sentence. Then replace it with a one-word verb.

> *e.g.* Keep back. The burning car is about to blow up. *Explode*

a My application to join the leadership team was turned down. ____________________

b Please turn off the burner when you finish the experiment. ____________________

c He has walked out on the project. ____________________

d The car sped up as it turned into the street. ____________________

e He's overcharged me. I've been ripped off. ____________________

f When did you find out about the error? ____________________

6 Underline the verb that agrees with the subject in the following sentences.

a Some senior students (has / have) private study periods.

b Aeroplanes (carries / carry) mail as well as passengers.

c Many people (visits / visit) the National War Memorial in Canberra.

d The team (hopes / hope) to secure a new sponsor next season.

e A team of white horses (was / were) pulling the carriage.

f An army of cleaners (has / have) rushed to clear away the wreckage.

7 Write S–V–O (subject–verb–object) or S–V–IO-DO (subject–verb–indirect object–direct object) in the answer spaces for each of the following sentences.

a He finished his assignment. ________________

b He lent me his assignment. ________________

c I will bake her a cake. ________________

d I will bake a cake this afternoon. ________________

e I showed the class my film. ________________

8 Underline the verb in each of the sentences below and write if it is active or passive.

a The police caught the bank robber. ________________

b The cat was chased by a dog. ________________

c The best essay was read aloud by the teacher. ________________

d A cricket crowd applauds good play by the home team and the opposition. ________________

e Precise nouns and active verbs are needed for good writing. ________________

Name: | Due date: | Guardian signature:

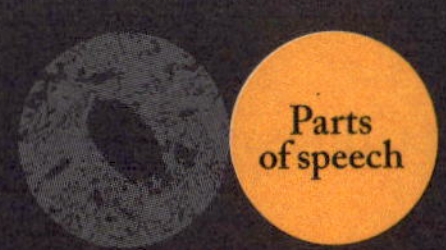

SPELLING FOCUS 1

Some people find spelling easy; for others, it is hard work. Different people use different strategies to learn to spell a word.

1 Underline three strategies below that work best for you. Answers will vary. Discuss the most effective strategies with a partner.

a The look-say-cover-write-check strategy.

b Writing the word out several times until you feel that you have mastered it.

c Visualising the word and its shape in your head.

d Saying the word and spelling it aloud several times.

e Asking someone to test you, while you either write the word down or spell it aloud.

f Noticing how the word is like or unlike another; for example, that *humorous* is like *humour* except that it drops the *u*, or that *caution* uses the *-tion* suffix that you see in other words.

g Breaking a word into its syllables before you try to spell it; for example, *ac/com/mo/da/tion.*

h Keeping a much-used personal spelling diary in which you record all the words that you find difficult.

i Using the spellchecker on your computer.

j Learning and regularly revising those spelling rules that work in English.

k Keeping a dictionary on hand whenever you are writing, and referring to it whenever you are in doubt, including using an online dictionary when you are writing on a computer.

l Looking for letter patterns in words and grouping words with similar patterns together, such as *thought, bought, fought.*

m Noticing how words are made up, so that you can identify root words, prefixes and suffixes; for example, *trans-* (common prefix), *-port-* (root word), *-ation* (common suffix).

n Having fun pronouncing a word the way it looks, as it should sound, such as pronouncing the *p* in words like *psychology* or the *k* in *knock.*

o Relying on memory aids or mnemonics for particularly tricky words, such as the BBC Schools website recommendation of 'O U lucky duck' if you have trouble with words like *could, should, would.*

p Paying particular attention to whatever is unusual about the spelling of a word, such as a silent letter or a doubling of letters.

2 **a** Every rule in the English language has exceptions. A widely known spelling rule is: *i* before *e* except after *c*. Write the correct *ei* or *ie* form in the blanks below.

dec☐☐ve	sc☐☐nce	h☐☐nous	surf☐☐t
rec☐☐ve	effic☐☐nt	s☐☐ze	v☐☐n
conc☐☐t	vacanc☐☐s	sh☐☐k	w☐☐r
consc☐☐nce	h☐☐ght	soc☐☐ty	w☐☐rd

b Many students remember '*i* before *e* except after *c*', but some forget the last part of the rule: it only works if the word rhymes with *be* or *see*. Underline the words in which *ie* or *ei* does not rhyme with *be*.

i neighbour	**v** veil	**ix** leisure	**xiii** priest
ii foreign	**vi** achieve	**x** shriek	**xiv** weight
iii believe	**vii** eight	**xi** height	
iv piece	**viii** thief	**xii** rein	

c Memorise these exceptions to the *ie* rule: *protein*, *weird*, *seize* and *weir*. Fill in the correct spellings in the gaps below.

It's w___rd that boys and girls need 1000 milligrams of calcium daily – the equivalent of 600 millilitres of skim milk, an egg and two sardines. Prot___n is another major component of bone health so I'll s___ze the day and follow a healthy diet.

3 While there are many irregularities in English spelling, fortunately there are some regular rules that we can learn or revise. Rewrite the verbs in the following table by adding *-ing* and *-ed*. Take care with the spelling.

	–ing	–ed
a step		
b bat		
c droop		
d drop		
e rob		
f whip		
g hop		
h seat		
i brim		
j star		
k reap		

Why do some words double the final letter when *-ing* or *-ed* are added, and others don't? Here is the rule to remember.

The rule for one-syllable words: the final consonant is doubled if the word has a single short vowel, such as *hop* and *rob*; if the one-syllable word contains two vowels, such as *droop* and *reap*, the final consonant is not doubled.

What happens when you add an -s to a noun ending in -y to make it plural?

The rule: if the letter before the -y is a *vowel* (a, e, i, o, u), you simply *add* -s (such as *guys*, *bays*, *alleys*). If the letter before the -y is a *consonant* (all letters that are not vowels), you change the -y to -i and add -es (for example *stories*, *allies*, *policies*).

4 Complete the blanks in the following plural nouns.

factories	store___ (building levels)	laundr___
turkeys	melod___	butterflies
stor___ (narratives)	toys	guys
dumm___	jock___	polic___
alleys	bays	balcon___

The rule for changing nouns ending in -y to plural is similar for verbs ending in -y when you add *-ed*: add *-ed* to each verb. Take care to change the -y to an -i where necessary.

5 Complete the blanks in the following table, adding *-ed* to the verbs.

	Verbs	-ed
a	enjoy	
b	marry	
c	play	
d	bury	
e	carry	
f	delay	
g	espy	
h	study	
i	try	
j	simplify	
k	cry	
l	obey	
m	employ	
n	defy	
o	annoy	

When you add *-ing* or *-ed* to a verb, what happens if the last letter of the verb is *e*?

The rule: when *-ing* or *-ed* are added to a verb ending in *e*, the *e* is dropped.

6 Complete the blanks in the following verbs. Cross out the *e* if you need to drop it.

practise	practising	practis___
exercise	exercise____	exercised
encourage	encourage____	encouraged
believe	believing	believ___
value	value____	valued
excite	excite____	excited
please	please____	pleased
divide	dividing	divid___

Language changes over time. Spelling has not changed a great deal since the invention of printing led to the standardisation of spelling, but some changes do occur, mostly for the better. There used to be complicated rules for nouns ending in *-o* when they were made plural: should they be spelt *-os* or *-oes*? The preference in modern spelling is *-os*, except for a short list of common words that are still spelt *-oes*. In many cases, *-os* and *-oes* are both correct. However, as *-os* is the modern preference, choose *-os*, except for those few words where only *-oes* is correct.

7 Underline in the table below the four common words that must be spelt *-oes*.

avocado	echo	photo	studio
banjo	ghetto	potato	tomato
buffalo	hero	radio	tornado
casino	mosquito	solo	torpedo
concerto	motto	soprano	volcano

8 Write the correct spelling next to each commonly misspelt word below.

Word	Answer	Word	Answer
recieve		metafor	
hight		similie	
wierd		humor	
naybour		psycology	
rythm		littrature	

Name:	Due date:	Guardian signature:

11 PERSONAL PRONOUNS

Parts of speech

A **pronoun** is a word used in place of a noun (*pro* means *for* the noun).
A **personal pronoun** is used in place of a noun that names people, animals or objects.

e.g. *You* can do *it*.
They told *me* to work steadily on *it*.

We usually label personal pronouns according to:

→ **person** (first person is the person speaking, second person is the person being spoken to, and third person is the person or thing being spoken about)
→ **gender** (male, female or thing)
→ **number** (singular – one, or plural – more than one).

	Singular		Plural	
	Subject	Object	Subject	Object
First person	I	me	we	us
Second person	you	you	you	you
Third person	he/she/it	him/her/it	they	them

These terms are also useful when learning another language. See Unit 9 if you are unclear about these forms.

1 Underline the pronouns in each sentence below.

- **a** The angler thought he'd caught the fish, but it got away.
- **b** Campers have fun because they tell stories and jokes next to a fire in winter.
- **c** 'You'll have to go with them to make sure they get there safely,' Mum told her.
- **d** 'Give it to me now!' she yelled to accept the pass to goal.
- **e** My grandparents took us to the market on Saturday morning. We loved it.
- **f** He looked at her in dismay.

2 Circle all the personal pronouns in the following passage. Then write the pronoun and specify the person and number. The first one has been done for you.

'I can't go yet. I told you, Marita, that I had a fall. They won't like it when I tell them I tripped on the sprinkler and accidentally broke the nozzle!'

I – first person singular;

Between you and me is correct because *me* is in the object position, after the preposition between. *Between you and I* is incorrect.

The noun that a pronoun replaces is called the referent. It is essential that the relationship between the noun and the pronoun is clear: we must know which noun a pronoun refers to if we want our writing and speech to be coherent.

1 Underline the pronoun that makes these sentences confusing.

- **a** If you try to load that game on your tablet, we can try it tonight.
- **b** Jemima kept in contact with Lisa after she changed schools.
- **c** Wei and Anna took their young cousins to the cinema and they said the cartoon characters were funny.
- **d** Kim ran to the sidelines to speak to her coach. She listened carefully.

2 Underline the five personal pronouns in the following school report on ICT.

How will we use digital technology? There is a wide choice of digital tools to use – it is already challenging for teachers to make effective and informed choices about what technology they use with junior secondary students. While it may be important to understand basic computer skills, we need to be able to promote students' future capabilities.

In polite speech and writing, put yourself *last* when including one or more persons.

e.g. Incorrect (impolite): Me, Jono and Ahmed are going to the footy.
Correct (polite): Jono, Ahmed and I are going to the footy.

3 It is important to use the correct forms of pronouns depending on whether they are in the subject or object position. Underline the pronoun that is used incorrectly in each of the following sentences and write the correct form of the pronoun in the space that follows.

- **a** Us Australians are very enthusiastic about Australia Day. ________
- **b** Australia Day is important to we Australians. ________
- **c** There is a close understanding between the President and I. ________
- **d** Me and her did the washing up. ________
- **e** Between you and I, we'd better leave now. ________
- **f** This will cause a disagreement between he and his friend. ________

4 Some students overuse the second person pronoun *you* in creative writing. Underline the second person pronouns in the following extract.

It was raining hard like you never saw before and all I wanted was to run as fast as I could to catch my regular train at the station nearest to school. Just when I was getting breathless – you know what it's like when you get careless and can't see properly – well, I slipped on the gushing gutter and fell flat on my face, dropping my computer bag in the gutter just outside the station entry for all to see. How would you feel then? I felt so embarrassed!

Name:	Due date:	Guardian signature:

12 ADJECTIVES

Parts of speech

An **adjective** is a word that describes a noun or pronoun and adds to the meaning of that noun or pronoun.

e.g. A *feral* cat is in the park.
They are *thirsty*.
Poetry in performance is *entertaining*.
Christmas is a *special* time of year for giving to *poor* people.

1 Underline the 12 adjectives in the following tourist promotion.

Tourists travel to Kangaroo Island to see the impressive wildlife. It's like visiting a huge natural zoo. Playful dolphins leap gracefully in front of the ferry as it pulls into the little harbour. A large colony of sea lions can be seen at Seal Bay. Many of the plump, lazy creatures lie on the broad expanse of the beach. Sleek, grey shapes can also be seen surfing in the rolling waves.

2 Complete the following passage with the appropriate adjectives from the box below.

Malvolio, a __________ butler with a __________ sense of humour, was trapped in a cellar and cried out to the servants of the house to release him from his __________ cell. They ignored his __________ cries for help and laughed at him with __________ jokes and __________ insults.

poor	dark	proud
stinging	desperate	teasing

3 In each pair of sentences that follow, underline the sentence in which the italicised word is used as an adjective (not as a noun).

a i He buys expensive *clothes*.
ii He buys a *clothes* brush.

b i Millionaires can now pay for *space* travel.
ii Some millionaires are prepared to pay to travel into *space*.

c i She is a *university* lecturer.
ii Her daughter goes to *university*.

d i Where do I go to take the *train*?
ii Where is the nearest *train* station?

e i Holidays can be useful for *study* courses.
ii Some students use the holidays for study.

Use a thesaurus to find more interesting synonyms for the adjectives you are using in your writing.

4 Underline the 11 adjectives in the following profile of a good teacher.

- → strong knowledge of the subject
- → enthusiastic communicator
- → good at exploring ideas with others
- → supportive team member and uses own initiative
- → caring person who enjoys working with diverse people
- → patient with a good sense of humour
- → open to change and challenges student thinking

1 Underline the 10 adjectives in the following brief student reflection on space exploration.

As technology increases, global collaboration between countries gives fresh hope to achieving new goals, such as sending a mission to Mars. Australia plays an important role in sharing and developing information through powerful telescopes. We don't know everything about the complex universe. The study of space is a dynamic subject. Perhaps better technology will help us to answer the big question: are we alone in the universe?

2 The English language is rich with synonyms – words of similar meaning. Draw lines to match the adjectives in column A with their synonyms in column B. Use your dictionary if you are not sure.

	Column A	Column B
a	sad	annoyed
b	glad	baffled
c	afraid	confused
d	embarrassed	dubious
e	muddled	frightened
f	puzzled	hopeful
g	doubtful	humiliated
h	optimistic	irate
i	irritated	pleased
j	furious	unhappy

3 Sort the 20 adjectives below into five groups, each one containing four synonyms. You may need to consult a dictionary to check the meaning of some words.

binding	halcyon	mistrusting	quiet
changeful	immaculate	moody	suspicious
compulsory	innocent	obligatory	temperamental
distrustful	mandatory	peaceful	tranquil
doubting	mercurial	pure	unblemished

a Group 1: ______________________

b Group 2: ______________________

c Group 3: ______________________

d Group 4: ______________________

e Group 5: ______________________

Name: | Due date: | Guardian signature:

13 ADJECTIVES: COMPARATIVES AND SUPERLATIVES

Parts of speech

Adjectives are often used to compare one object or person with another.

→ When we compare *two* nouns or pronouns, we use the **comparative** form.

e.g. He is *more active* than his friend. (two compared)

She is *more academic* than her brother. (two compared)

→ When we compare *three* or more nouns or pronouns, we use the **superlative** form.

e.g. He is the *most active* of the group. (three or more compared)

She is the *most academic* in the class. (three or more compared)

→ Short adjectives (two syllables or fewer) use an *–er* ending for the comparative form and an *–est* ending for the superlative.

e.g. I am *taller* than my best friend. (two compared)

You are the *tallest* in the class. (three or more compared)

Sometimes sports commentators misuse the superlative (perhaps out of enthusiasm):

e.g. The Wallabies were the *best* team today, simply magnificent.

If only two (comparative) teams were playing, it should be:

e.g. The Wallabies were the *better* team today, simply magnificent.

1 Read the following review of an SUV (sports utility vehicle). Underline the comparative adjectives and circle the superlatives.

> The new version has more cabin space and a bigger footprint for better handling and ride. As a top-range version, the generous equipment level is one of the best in its class.

2 In the spaces below, use the appropriate comparative or superlative form of the adjective in brackets.

a Who is the ________________ (bright) in the class?

b Who is the ________________ (bright) of the twins?

c Who is the ________________ (academic) in the class?

d Who is the ________________ (academic) of the twins?

e Which member of the team is the ________________ (fast)?

f Which of the two swimmers is the ________________ (fast)?

g Which member of the team is the ________________ (successful)?

h Which of the two swimmers is the ________________ (successful)?

Remember the adjective *unique*, meaning 'one of its kind', cannot be compared.

There are some exceptions to the standard comparative and superlative forms of adjectives. The table below lists the most common exceptions. Memorise the five comparative and superlative adjectives.

Adjective	Comparative	Superlative
good	better	best
bad	worse	worst
many	more	most
much/some	more	most
little	less	least

1 Use the table above to help you choose the appropriate comparative or superlative form of the adjective in brackets.

a My breaststroke is ________ (good) than my butterfly stroke.

b My cold was bad yesterday and, unfortunately, it is ________ (bad) today.

c Our class raised the ________ (much) money.

d My teacher encouraged me to put ________ (much) effort into my writing.

e Cathy achieved 80 per cent - her ________ (good) ever maths score.

f Hanako has read ________ (much) books than I have.

g The ________ (good) thing about listening to iTunes is the huge range of choices.

h Yoghurt is ________ (good) than ice-cream.

i Two out of three is the ________ (good) I can do.

j I chose a left rather than a right turn but that made my overall time ________ (bad) than yours.

English usage changes over time. An example of change is the confusing use of *fewer* and *less*. The traditional rule for formal writing and speech is that *fewer* is used with **plural nouns of number** (*fewer people*, *fewer examples*), while *less* is used with **singular nouns of quantity** (*less sugar*, *less noise*). Remember that in informal speech *less* tends to be used for both number and quantity.

2 Write *fewer* for number or *less* for quantity in the following sentences.

a There are ____________ young people in country towns because jobs are scarce.

b There is ____________ youth in country towns because jobs are scarce.

c I suggest you use ____________ raisins in that recipe.

d I suggest you use ____________ sugar in that recipe.

e There was ____________ immigration last year.

f There were ____________ immigrants last year.

Name:	Due date:	Guardian signature:

14 ADVERBS

Parts of speech

An **adverb** usually adds meaning to a verb. To identify the adverb in a sentence, ask *how?*, *where?* or *when?* after a verb. Many adverbs end with the suffix –*ly*.

e.g. Susie danced *gracefully*.
Question: danced *how*?
Answer: *gracefully* (adverb)

Sometimes adverbs add meaning to an adjective or another adverb.

e.g. The music was played *too* loudly.
She is *very* happy with the result.

Note that not all adverbs end with the suffix –*ly*.

e.g. How are you going?
Good, thanks. (colloquial reply; *good* usually used as an adjective)

In polite and formal speech, the answer is: *Well*, thanks. (adverb)

1 Write the adverbs for the following adjectives.

	Adjective	Adverb
a	quick	
b	happy	
c	wise	
d	weary	
e	pretty	
f	horrible	
g	brave	
h	feeble	
i	impulsive	
j	easy	
k	sharp	
l	attentive	

Take care not to use an adjective when an adverb is needed: *He plays well* (not *good*). *I'm doing well* (not *good*). Note that informal speech substitutes the adverb *well* with the adjective *good*.

2 Underline the adverbs in the following sentences.

- **a** Alphonse sang beautifully.
- **b** I nearly fainted when I crossed the finishing line.
- **c** The key forward played poorly in the final.
- **d** He fought bravely.
- **e** I practised sluggishly tonight.

3 Underline the five adverbs in the following reflection on 'wellness' electives.

> I started courses in stained glass, yoga and meditation. I worked hard at each course, listened intently and practised regularly, and, fortunately, I became more confident in making good choices. I said to myself, 'I'm gradually seeing what's good for me.'

Some adverbs tell us *how* something happened (adverbs of manner), *when* something happened (adverbs of time) or *where* something happened (adverbs of place).

1 Underline the adverbs in the sentences below and then write *adverb of manner, time* or *place* after each sentence.

- **a** The whole team played harmoniously. ______________________
- **b** I'm not feeling well. It must be something I ate. ______________________
- **c** Sometimes after school I go to a mate's house. ______________________
- **d** Whenever I do this card trick, someone always asks me how I did it. ______________________
- **e** He reluctantly accepted the gift. ______________________
- **f** At lunchtime I usually hang around with my friends. ______________________
- **g** There were people everywhere on the beach. ______________________
- **h** Put your test paper there, please. ______________________

2 Write the adverbs for the following adjectives by adding *–ly*. Take care with the spelling. Use your dictionary if you are uncertain about the correct spelling.

	Adjective	Adverb
a	satisfactory	
b	believable	
c	beautiful	
d	necessary	
e	romantic	
f	simple	

	Adjective	Adverb
g	frantic	
h	primary	
i	helpful	
j	considerable	
k	careful	
l	close	

Name: Due date: Guardian signature:

REVISION TEST 3

1 Underline the 11 personal pronouns below. Above each pronoun write S for singular or P for plural.

a We'll have fun swimming with the first graders and helping them practise their strokes.

b The coach advised the key forward, 'Bounce it, run with it and you will lose them.'

c The girl stared at the dog. He barked at her, then she watched him run across the park.

d You will need medical attention.

2 For each pronoun that you identified in exercise 1, write what person it is and whether it is the subject or the object.

e.g. We – first person, subject

______________________ ______________________

______________________ ______________________

______________________ ______________________

______________________ ______________________

______________________ ______________________

3 Underline the 12 adjectives in the following descriptive fantasy piece.

Gobbo was an ugly toad with green, pimply skin, a wart on his droopy nose and yellow, decayed teeth. The poor thing looked unhappy, so I invited the little creature into the front garden. He was scared and he tried to hide behind a large fern.

4 Write the correct comparative or superlative adjective in the space provided. The first letter in the blank is a clue.

a The weather is m_______ reliable in Sydney than in Melbourne.

b The drought is w_______ in the country than in the city.

c I find the vegetables are b_______ in the market than in the supermarket.

d The b_______ quality strawberries and cherries are not always the m_______ expensive.

e The top runner scored the h_______ metabolic and acceleration rates in the team.

5 Underline the five adverbs in the following reflection on a children's food course.

I now move about easily and comfortably in the kitchen because I can choose herbs and vegetables from the garden and try out recipes. They turn out well. I have to calculate all the portions carefully. It's great greedily eating homemade oatmeal cookies and drinking fresh orange juice when the cooking is done.

6 Underline the correct form of the comparative or superlative adjective.

a The criminal's behaviour is the worse / worst in the state's history.
b Low-fat yoghurt is better / best than ice-cream.
c The weather turned hotter / hottest after September.
d Two out of three is the better / best I can do.
e My overall time was worse / worst than yours.

7 Change these adjectives into adverbs.

	Adjective	Adverb
a	sad	
b	pretty	
c	romantic	
d	good	
e	fruitful	
f	total	
g	hungry	
h	frantic	
i	emphatic	
j	charitable	
k	noisy	
l	skilful	
m	pitiful	
n	attractive	
o	sure	
p	whole	
q	loyal	

8 Underline the adverbs in the sentences below. Then write whether it is an *adverb of manner, time or place.*

a He lives nearby. ____________________
b We left them behind. ____________________
c I will text my mother soon. ____________________
d They were walking quickly. ____________________
e The storm is close. ____________________
f The audience applauded enthusiastically. ____________________
g I ran fast. ____________________
h I used to run there every afternoon. ____________________
i I used to run daily. ____________________

Name:	Due date:	Guardian signature:

15 PREPOSITIONS

Parts of speech

A **preposition** shows the positioning relationship between people, things and actions. Here are some words that can be used as prepositions:

above	beside	from	through
across	between	in	to
after	by	of	under
at	down	on	up
before	for	over	with

Note that some of the words in the table above can be parts of speech other than prepositions; for example, *before* and *after* are commonly used as linking words. You can only determine the part of speech of a word by the way in which it is used in a sentence. If a sentence sounds strange to you (many people don't like *us Australians*, even when it is used grammatically in the object position), rephrase it. For example, instead of saying: 'It's a secret between you and me', rephrase it as: 'It's our secret.'

HAVE A GO

1 Complete the following sentences with an appropriate preposition.

- **a** The water __________ the pool was freezing.
- **b** We shall keep this a secret __________ the two of us.
- **c** New York differs greatly __________ Dehli.
- **d** I prefer the guitar __________ the violin.
- **e** I usually go __________ bed __________ ten o'clock.
- **f** I last saw the old man standing __________ the river.
- **g** Stephie prefers netball __________ basketball.
- **h** The dog dug __________ the fence.
- **i** Did you know that someone has rowed __________ the Atlantic Ocean?

2 Remember to identify the part of speech of a word when it is used in a sentence. Write five appropriate prepositions in the following blanks.

> The market has been trading ______ half a century and is the hub ______ the central shopping area, ______ many cafés and restaurants. It's popular ______ locals and visitors ______ all backgrounds.

You can only identify the part of speech of a word when it is used in a sentence.

3 Add the appropriate preposition to these sentences.

a He was acquitted __________ the crime.

b She is confident __________ her own ability.

c I don't like the way they gloat __________ their victory.

d I develop confidence __________ doing public speaking.

e Write __________ black or blue pen.

f Babies are immunised __________ a range of diseases.

g The young man was initiated __________ the tribe.

h She comments constructively __________ my handwriting.

i He embarked __________ a career in journalism.

j Take __________ this challenge.

k Are you acquainted __________ his brother?

l I take tour images __________ my smartphone.

4 Underline the seven prepositions in the following horoscope.

Is your secret formula to success buried in a safe? Do you see when a sign of good fortune comes across your path? Do not worry about little things. Share your life with others and this week will bring sunshine into your heart!

A **prepositional phrase** contains a preposition and a noun or pronoun.

e.g. *in the park, under the house, through the woods, with them, from you, to me*

The noun or pronoun in the prepositional phrase is in the object position.

Underline the correct form of personal pronoun to complete the following sentences. Remember that a pronoun that comes after a preposition is in the object position.

a This financial agreement insures you and (I / me) against loss.

b Eating a banana a day is good for you and (I / me).

c For Brad, Louis and (he / him), the win was special.

d For (we / us) Australians, the arts and sport are passionate pursuits.

e He will make the presentation to you and (I / me).

f We sent condolences on behalf of (we / us) members.

Name: | Due date: | Guardian signature:

16 DETERMINERS

Parts of speech

Nouns are often preceded by the words *the*, *a* or *an*, called **determiners**.

The determiner *the* is called the **definite article**. It is used before both singular and plural nouns.

Give me *the* answers, please.

She took *the* ball.

The Prime Minister addressed *the* nation.

The **indefinite article** *a* is used with singular nouns; *an* is used when the singular noun begins with a vowel sound.

Give me *an* answer, please.

She took *a* ball from the kit.

A prime minister addresses the nation when *an* important issue arises requiring *a* decisive response.

Note that the decision to use *an* depends on the sound; it is often used before a word beginning with *h*, but not before *history*.

an indefinite article

an hour

an honest mistake

an hotel

a union

a 7-seater SUV

a once-in-a-lifetime achievement

Many small, functional words that were classified as types of adjective in traditional grammar are now usually called determiners.

→ demonstrative adjectives – *this, that, these, those*

→ possessive adjectives – *my, your, his, her, its, our, their*

→ quantitative adjectives – *few, both, some, each, every, all*

1 Underline the correct determiner in the following sentences.

- **a** As the monarch's reign comes to an end, an / a heir is chosen.
- **b** It takes half a / an hour to queue for discount tickets.
- **c** I plan to go to an / a university where Arts and Law are offered.
- **d** She starts her day with a breakfast consisting of a / an egg, a / an orange and a / an banana.

It is the sound of the word that follows, not the spelling, that determines whether we use *a* or *an*.

2 Circle the word from the list that best fits the sentence.

a The council bought a heritage house with an ______________ garden.

colourful | lovely | exquisite | gorgeous

b I want you to give me a ______________ opinion.

honest | frank | immediate | unbiased

c I read my little brother an ______________ story.

scary | funny | ghost | amusing

d Are you planning an ______________ to the show?

visit | trip | excursion | journey

e An ______________ of scientists will travel to Antarctica.

expedition | group | band | number

f He could see nothing but a ______________ future ahead.

bleak | ominous | inauspicious | unfavourable

g It was a ______________ rescue.

excellent | audacious | daring | intrepid

h He spent a ______________ evening.

unpleasant | undesirable | disagreeable | obnoxious

You can only tell what part of speech a word is when it is used in context. The determiners *this, that, these* and *those* can also be used as pronouns. When they are used as determiners they come before a noun.

e.g. *that* old house, *these* stairs

When they are used as pronouns they replace the noun.

e.g. Do you see the old house on the corner? *That* is where I used to live. (*That* refers to *house*.)

Wooden stairs can become rickety. *These* need replacing. (*These* refers to *stairs*.)

Look at the use of *this, that, these* and *those* in the following sentences. Underline the ones that are used as determiners (before a noun).

a I have to give these books to the librarian.

b Leave the books on the desk. Those are overdue.

c Put those roses into the pink vase and cut the stems of these yellow roses.

d His roses are stunning this year.

e See the painting on the back wall. That is mine.

f That painting is part of my major project for the exam.

g Carry one kit at a time. Give me those.

h Those kits have to be carried to the oval.

Name: | Due date: | Guardian signature:

17 PHRASES

Parts of speech

A **phrase** is a group of words without a finite verb. (A finite verb is a verb that has a subject.)

e.g. *After the rain*, the girls played.

After the rain (phrase = no finite verb) is not a sentence but it tells you when the girls played.

A phrase often starts with a preposition (see Unit 15), such as *after*, *above*, *at*, *despite*, *of*, *under*, *since* or *between*.

e.g. *Since the old days*, my family has farmed.
The baby crawled *under the table.*

1 Underline the phrase(s) in each sentence below.

- **a** She lay on the sofa.
- **b** After a long look, Paddy closed the door behind him.
- **c** Mai stood on the table.
- **d** The baby crawled under the table.

A phrase can start with a participle (see Unit 5).

e.g. *Watching* carefully, she calculated each move.
Caught on video, the player had no excuse.

While prepositional phrases and participial phrases are the most common, a phrase can be any group of words that belong together as long as there is no finite verb. A phrase can appear anywhere in a sentence. There can be more than one phrase in a sentence, but a phrase is always a group of words that makes a unit of meaning and belongs together, not just any string of unrelated words.

e.g. *One of several wounded*, my great grandfather luckily survived the war.

2 Underline the phrase in each sentence below.

- **a** Waiting my turn, I tried to work out my opponent's strategy.
- **b** Abandoned by its mother, the kitten managed to survive till it was rescued.
- **c** The car stalled, stranding its passengers.
- **d** My brother, running wildly, brushed a tree branch.
- **e** Lost in thought, he forgot to make sufficient time for a written conclusion.

Phrases are groups of words that belong together but do not have a verb with a subject.

1 Choose the best phrase from the options below to complete each sentence.

holding the door open	keen to research information
on the large canvas	over the fence
down the leafy avenue	armed with maps and timetables

a He wandered ____.

b She opened her device, ____.

c The rabbit sprung ____.

d ____, I slid the tray into the oven.

e ____, they made their plan.

f ____, she drew a picture.

2 Some explorers are remembered in plaques and monuments. Underline the phrases in the following student journal.

Captain Charles Sturt is said to have marked a tree on the site of the memorial at Narrandera. He was excited and wrote that his journey was made through 'fine country and along a beautiful river'. After a river full of fish, he viewed a big plain, which he named after his surgeon Hamilton. Sturt led a small group of soldiers and convicts through the area, near the end of 1829. He continued his epic journey along the Murrumbidgee River.

3 Underline four participial phrases in the following transition guide.

With their children's best interests at heart, parents can work in partnership with teachers, enabling a smooth transition for their child in the first year of secondary school. Additional to email and phone contact, a person-to-person meeting is welcome. After a parent–teacher interview, parents can help promote open communication and realistic expectations through the early months of Year 7.

4 Underline the seven participial phrases in the following pre-game report.

With a bumper crowd and enthusiasm galore, expectations of both sides are high. For a match to be competitive to the end, both sides must play hard and have fun doing it. With solid finals' experience and lists with a lot of depth, both sides match up well through all the statistics and frequent strategy sessions. In high-pressure situations, the star quality rises to the surface, however hot the pressure, and the forward line of each team, near the end of the third quarter, will receive the most scrutiny of fans and coaches alike. Behind all the hype, both teams know they have a job to do and the skills to achieve grand final success.

Name: | Due date: | Guardian signature:

18 CLAUSES

Parts of speech

A **clause** is a group of words that contains a subject and a verb. There are two types of clause: the main (or independent) clause and the subordinate (or dependent) clause.

A **main clause** usually makes complete sense on its own and expresses the main message of the sentence.

e.g. The skiers raced in twilight.

Sentences can have more than one main clause. These clauses are joined by linking words such as *and* and *but*.

e.g. (The party noise continued) (*and* the neighbours complained.)
main clause — main clause

When you have two (or more) main clauses of equal value, they are called **coordinate clauses**. A clause must have a verb with a subject.

1 Each sentence below has two coordinate clauses. Put brackets around each clause and underline the word that joins them.

e.g. The bells were ringing and the lights shone brightly.
(The bells were ringing) <u>and</u> (the lights shone brightly.)

a I like ice-cream but my sister prefers chocolate.
b The spaceship took off and then it vanished.
c I read the paper online but you might like reading the sports blog.
d The ferry docked and the passengers disembarked.
e A car hit the power pole and the whole area was blacked out.
f You can finish your work here or you can take it to the library.

A **subordinate clause** is not as important as the main clause in a sentence. It is a dependent clause that offers extra information but cannot stand alone. An introductory word such as *if*, *that*, *when* or *because* introduces a subordinate clause.

e.g. (The cyclists raced in twilight) (because they were risk-takers.)
main clause — subordinate clause

The subordinate clause gives extra information about the main clause.

(When you have finished your work), (you should go to the library.)
subordinate clause — main clause

A clause must have a verb with a subject.

2 Put brackets around the main clauses and underline the subordinate clauses in the following sentences.

> *e.g.* (My writing is better) because I put more effort into drafting my ideas.

- **a** The batter hit another century while the selectors watched admiringly.
- **b** This is the house in which my dad was born.
- **c** Unless people give to charity, poor families will suffer.
- **d** Jenny was sure that Sarah was planning a surprise party for her.
- **e** I decided to take public transport home since the service is frequent and reliable.
- **f** Because their skills needed more attention, the students sat a practice test.

3 A clause must have a verb with a subject. Underline the verbs in the following sentences and draw an arrow from the verb to its subject.

- **a** The batter hit another century while the selectors watched admiringly.
- **b** This is the house in which my dad was born.
- **c** Unless people give to charity, poor families will suffer.
- **d** Jenny was sure that Sarah was planning a surprise party for her.
- **e** I decided to take public transport home since the service is frequent and reliable.
- **f** Because their skills needed more attention, the students sat a practice test.

In each pair of sentences below, one sentence consists of just one main clause; the other has a second clause. Underline the sentences that have more than one clause.

a
- i Because of the storm, the whole area was blacked out.
- ii Because the storm was destructive, the whole area was blacked out.

b
- i After the drought, the farmers rejoiced at the substantial rain.
- ii After the drought had broken, the farmers rejoiced at the substantial rain.

c
- i Jenny was happy that Rema had finalised her plans.
- ii Jenny was happy about Rema's plans.

d
- i This is a man of distinction.
- ii This is a man who has won distinction.

e
- i I have read five books since the Christmas holidays began.
- ii I have read five books since the beginning of the Christmas holidays.

f
- i The man in the green car was responsible for the accident.
- ii The man driving the green car was responsible for the accident.

g
- i This book, which is a favourite of mine, was given to me for my fifth birthday.
- ii One of my favourite books was given to me for my thirteenth birthday.

Name: | Due date: | Guardian signature:

19 COORDINATING CONJUNCTIONS

Parts of speech

Conjunctions are joining words. They are used to join words, phrases and clauses.

e.g. A balance of work *and* play is essential for a healthy life.
Take the path down the hill *but* don't run on the gravel.
I go home early on Wednesdays *either* to practise basketball *or* prepare my essay.

Coordinating conjunctions *and*, *but* and *or* join words, phrases and clauses that have equal value or status.

The most common coordinating conjunctions are *and*, *but*, *either* … *or*, *neither* … *nor* and *yet*.

1 Choose from the conjunctions *and*, *but*, *or*, *nor* and *yet* to complete the following sentences.

- **a** You can use apples __________ oranges to make a mixed fruit drink.
- **b** Fluffy bolted across the road __________ up a tree.
- **c** I like going out __________ staying home is also relaxing.
- **d** We had four different cereals __________ no milk!
- **e** I tried again __________ again __________ I wasn't selected for the blue team.
- **f** He helped with the project, __________ he assumed he could do less than others.
- **g** The actor has neither fine features __________ an appealing voice.
- **h** You can complete a course __________ you need to learn more skills on the job.
- **i** Do the extra work __________ you may be disappointed with your final performance.

2 Underline the coordinating conjunctions in the following sentences.

- **a** Maria sent her application for class representative and waited for her teacher's response.
- **b** I checked the weather report and packed some thermals for the trip.
- **c** Melbourne is classified as a highly liveable city but its public transport needs upgrading.
- **d** You can put in more effort or suffer disappointment with your results.
- **e** Queensland is often seen as either a tourist attraction or an investment opportunity.
- **f** I can wait longer for you yet I feel you could do more in less time.
- **g** The spectators protested loudly yet they expected the referee to decide in their favour.
- **h** Neither my sister nor my brother played the violin.

Use coordinating conjunctions to join two or more main clauses.

1 Underline the five coordinating conjunctions in the following study guide for high school students.

- → Use highlighters to mark the key points in a book review or to identify important quotes to learn by heart for the exam.
- → Circle your errors in spelling words or mistakes in multiplications that you find difficult to process.
- → Tick off the task instructions with a pen or cross them off with a highlighter to check you have completed all parts of the assignment.
- → Use sticky notes to remind you what to take home and what to bring back to school.
- → Use sticky notes to write down your questions about a text study or your personal thoughts on characters.

2 Use coordinating conjunctions to join two or more main clauses. Choose an appropriate conjunction to join each pair of sentences below into one sentence with two clauses.

a I wanted to catch the train. There was track work. Only buses were running.

b I was keen to see the film. I had to look after my little brother and sister.

c The swimmer stood on the blocks. She looked intently at the end of her lane.

d I was hoping to catch them before they left. They had already gone by the time I arrived.

e I have two subjects for homework. I have enough time after dinner to complete both assignments.

f I read novels for pleasure. I read other literature and texts online for more information and self-knowledge.

Name:	Due date:	Guardian signature:

20 SUBORDINATING CONJUNCTIONS

Parts of speech

Subordinating conjunctions join dependent or subordinate clauses to the main clause. They include:

after	as
before	where
although	because
since	while
when	until

e.g. ***As*** **my coach told me, the centre player makes proper position for forward play.**
I arrive early at school *because* my mother drops me off on her way to work.
Can I see you *when* the match is over?

Note: some words that are used as conjunctions can also be used as prepositions. You can only identify the part of speech of a word when it is used in a sentence.

1 Join each pair of sentences below with the conjunction provided to make one sentence with two clauses.

e.g. The cat was a friendly ginger one. It disliked my dog. (although)
Answer: The cat was a friendly ginger one, *although* it disliked my dog.

a Dimita was a kind person. She raised money for special needs. (because)

b *Les Misérables* enjoyed box-office success on stage. The musical was made into a film. (after)

c The cyclists were riding along the track. They swerved to avoid a cat. (when)

d She was frustrated. She wanted to help her mum through her grief. (because)

e How can I finish my homework? You expect me to wash up tonight. (when)

Subordinating conjunctions join dependent clauses to the main clause.

2 Underline the subordinating conjunctions in the following sentences.

- **a** After they arrived at the party, the guests were introduced to my parents.
- **b** Although I like cake and ice-cream, I've decided to eat fruit for dessert to get fit.
- **c** Since she's been supporting me, I've felt much more confident.
- **d** I like cricket when it's tense and unpredictable.
- **e** There is no room for lateness since the exam starts on time.
- **f** When I'm mindful of others, I listen.
- **g** We feel lost on a restless sea when we hear bad news.
- **h** Because I could not stop, I left behind all care of consequences.

Sentences can be linked (although not combined) by adverbs (sometimes called conjunctive adverbs or text connectives). These linking words, which make connections, are very important in giving coherence to language. They include:

consequently	finally
first(ly)	however
second(ly)	nevertheless
third(ly)	therefore
moreover	thus

He loved the film. *However*, I was bored.

We have quite different tastes. *Nevertheless*, I will go to the movies with him again.

We have great times together; *therefore*, I can put up with the occasional boring movie.

Note that these sentences are linked but not combined into one sentence. They are separated by a full stop or, sometimes, by a semicolon.

Underline the four adverbs that are used as linking words in the following student letter to the editor.

Dear Sir/Madam

The recent article on the national survey that states children spend four hours a weekend, on average, on screens (tablets, other digital devices and TV) is cause for concern. Consequently, parents and schools need to give this screen addiction more attention. First, my parents and I believe there should be a balance with the arts, music and sport – active forms of mental and social engagement. Second, passive entertainment or distraction is not good for growing brains. Third, more time is better spent reading and talking with one's family rather than allowing a young head to stare at a screen at the meal table.

Yours sincerely

Melissa 13 years old

Name: Due date: Guardian signature:

REVISION TEST 4

1 Complete the following sentences with an appropriate preposition.

a He was accompanied __________ a concerned officer.

b I am not to blame __________ the problem.

c She likes to haggle __________ the price of goods at the market.

d Children need to be immunised __________ measles.

e My uncle gives advice __________ my studies.

f Are you satisfied __________ your results?

g I was encouraged __________ his praise.

h I can rely __________ your support.

2 **a** Underline the coordinating conjunctions and circle the subordinating conjunctions in the following report.

Yoga, which she started to help her relax and lose weight after her mother died, helps her to appreciate her body's flexibility and strength when she feels tired. She focuses on balance and healthy choices but sees yoga as fun because it is part of a journey to face life's challenges.

b Add the appropriate conjunction (coordinating and subordinating) in the following paragraph on Chinese culture.

Chinese Moon Festival is celebrated __________ the 15th __________ the eighth lunar month. The festival is held __________ the moon is at its brightest __________ roundest. The moon symbolises unity; consequently family members will gather to celebrate, eat mooncakes __________ light lanterns. The festival includes entertainment and a lion dancing performance.

3 In each pair of sentences below, one sentence consists of one main clause; the other has a second clause. Underline each sentence that has more than one clause.

a i After the storm, the whole area was blacked out.

ii After the storm swept through the region, the whole area was blacked out.

b i Because of the drought, food prices have increased.

ii Because the state has been in drought, food prices have increased.

c i Giovanni was quite sad about Maria's unexpected announcement.

ii Giovanni was quite sad that Maria had made such an unexpected announcement.

d i Do you know the woman who is driving the old utility?

ii Do you know the woman driving the old utility?

e i He shouted for help as he ran towards the neighbour's house.

ii Shouting for help, he ran towards the neighbour's house.

2 As you can see from the previous examples, sometimes – but not always – embedded clauses are contained within commas. The use of commas can change the meaning. To see the differences in the pairs of sentences below, you might find it helpful to read them aloud, listening to the way the commas affect the meaning.

a Underline the sentence that means that all soldiers are likely to run away.

i Soldiers, who run away, are not welcome in my army.

ii Soldiers who run away are not welcome in my army.

b Underline the sentence that means that accommodation is not available to teenagers.

i I will not let rooms to teenagers who play loud music all night.

ii I will not let rooms to teenagers, who play loud music all night.

c Underline the sentence that means that all politicians are liars.

i Politicians, who tell lies, deserve the public's contempt.

ii Politicians who tell lies deserve the public's contempt.

Underline the embedded clauses in the following paragraphs.

a

My aunt, who leaned on her elbow on the little round table that she usually kept beside her, eyed him attentively. My sister's new boyfriend who was from interstate was being carefully evaluated. I was nervous, as the introduction felt strangely awkward, yet I managed to talk sociably with Abdul.

b

"My name (Percy) which is an uncommon name means perseverance, and persevering to reach my goal of becoming a published author is something I am very proud of.

I write poetry which is a special craft because I want to encourage and motivate other young adults to follow their dreams and persevere no matter what life throws at them."

Percy Shodzi, who grew up in South Africa, will officially launch his latest collection at a free event at The Way Church, Vermont on Saturday, February 18, at 3 p.m.

c

Chocolate has long been associated with love, so it's the perfect time for *Teenage Chocolate, The Recipes* to be released, just in time for Valentine's Day. Eighteen-year-old entrepreneur Ronnie Wild who also plays guitar in a rock band certainly struck oil when he discovered raw chocolate soon after a revelation at 15 in his Year 9 Home Economics class when he decided: "I would find what I wanted to do and do it my way."

Three years of hard work has put him at the pivotal point for start-up success. *Teenage Chocolate*, a company with a national reach of 400 stockists in all states, is testimony to his vision, belief and authenticity.

Ronnie Wild, who is his own best brand ambassador, comes from humble origins. His parents backed him and his school supported his enterprising ideas to make the highest quality chocolate for the teenage market.

He doesn't just talk up his products, which are delicious to sample, and its message of doing good as a teenager – he lives it.

Name:	Due date:	Guardian signature:

22 SENTENCES (1)

Phrases, clauses and sentences

A **fragmentary sentence** is a set of words punctuated to look like a sentence but not a grammatically complete sentence.

e.g. The race. My destiny.

These are phrases, not sentences, because they do not have finite verbs. In this case you can add a verb to create one sentence:

e.g. *The race was my destiny.* (verb = *was*)

The example that follows has a finite verb, *lost*, but it is a subordinate or dependent clause.

e.g. When the champion lost the race.

It is a fragmentary sentence because it needs a main clause to be a sentence:

e.g. When the champion lost the race, the crowd was disappointed.

The next example has a finite verb, *didn't tell*, but it is a subordinate or dependent clause.

e.g. Because he didn't tell me the truth.

It is a fragmentary sentence because it needs a main clause to be a proper sentence:

e.g. I'm reluctant to trust him again because he didn't tell me the truth.

Some professional writers use fragmentary sentences skilfully for dramatic effect. It is fun to experiment with fragmentary sentences, but unwise to use them in your writing for assessment.

Fragmentary sentences are used regularly in conversation, and you can make dialogue in your narrative more realistic by using them.

e.g. 'Do you feel happy?'
'Not really.'

1 Rewrite each fragmentary sentence as a grammatically complete sentence or sentences. You will need to add a finite verb.

e.g. Winning: The siren. Victory.
Answer: The siren sealed our victory. (verb = *sealed*)

a Outside! Right now.

b Oh, the rainbow. How beautiful.

c What a night!

A sentence must have a main clause with a finite verb.

d In through the back door, up the stairs and straight to bed.

e Something glistening in the dark. The blade of a knife? The barrel of a gun?

2 Rewrite the following sentences and integrate any fragmentary sentences.

a The student assembly was enthralled. Listening to the famous guest speaker.

b The class was working quietly. Apart from the boys in the back row.

c Some students complained. There had been too much homework lately.

d When the bell rings. You are expected to move to your classrooms. In an orderly fashion.

e The computer was not working. Because it was not plugged in.

TAKE IT FURTHER

As mentioned on the previous page, there are times when a fragmentary sentence can be used for dramatic effect. Underline each fragmentary sentence below.

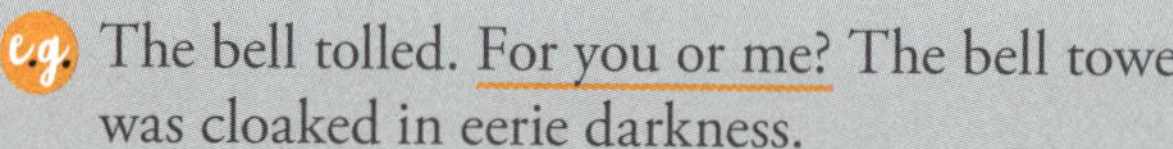

e.g. The bell tolled. For you or me? The bell tower was cloaked in eerie darkness.

a The door. It's wide open. My neighbour wouldn't have left it like that when she went on holiday. I think I hear noise from inside. Go inside and check? Not an easy decision.

b They're at the starting line. This time, Majid. The championship comes down to your event. Pressure on. Good luck, mate.

c Tash's mother couldn't believe the mess in her teenage daughter's room. Rubbish and clothes everywhere. She shut the door. What a disgrace! An insult to the whole family.

Name: | Due date: | Guardian signature:

23 SENTENCES (2)

Phrases, clauses and sentences

A **run-on sentence** adds to another when it really should be kept separate.

e.g. I struggled to keep afloat the lifesaver eventually reached me far from the shore I was overcome with relief that I had been rescued.

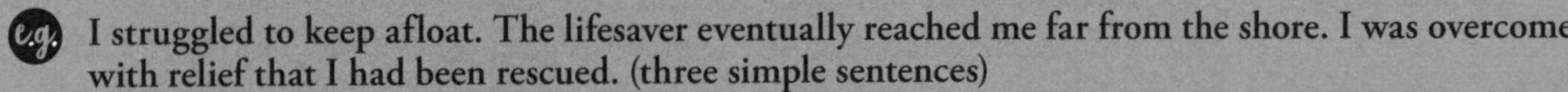

This is better written as:

e.g. I struggled to keep afloat. The lifesaver eventually reached me far from the shore. I was overcome with relief that I had been rescued. (three simple sentences)

To correct run-on sentences, you need to decide on the number of simple sentences and where to put the full stop. Remember to start the next sentence with a capital letter.

1 Correct the following run-on sentences by rewriting them, adding the full stops where they are needed. Remember to begin each new sentence with a capital letter.

a At the circus we saw the clowns and trapeze artists I especially liked the tightrope-walker.

b We had a great time at Luna Park and really enjoyed the rides I got tired after walking around for a few hours I wanted to go home but the others hadn't yet spent their money.

c First he went to the skateboard park to see if Tom was there then he decided to try the local shopping mall however, he had no luck in the end he thought he might as well go home and wait for Tom to turn up when he was ready.

d When the puppy saw a kitten, he escaped under the table she was only trying to be playful in Bindy's mind the tiny kitten had had been confused with a raging tiger.

Reading your work aloud can help you to decide whether you need a full stop or a comma.

When correcting run-on sentences you may wish to add conjunctions, such as *and*, *but*, or *who*, to link some sentences.

e.g. We enjoyed the Grand Prix, I tired after walking around for a few hours and wanted to go home and have a sleep.

Answer: We enjoyed the Grand Prix but I tired after walking around for a few hours. I wanted to go home and have a sleep.

Underline the right conjunction to correct the following run-on sentence in this advertisement.

a

FATHER'S DAY PRIZES

This Father's Day, help Dad be the healthiest dad he can be by winning him Tiger Kazan's prize pack (and / that) a T-shirt, (who / but) don't delay (who / as) there will be a huge rush for this super offer.

b

PANELBEATER

$80,000 PLUS

We are a reliable, high-quality and unique vehicle repair shop (who / that) provides exceptional service for our customers (whom / who) we totally care about. We are looking for a qualified panelbeater (and / who) takes pride in their work. Must also have great attention to detail, good communication skills (but / and) be well presented for our panel shop based in Coolangatta.

Call Mickey 0413 017 123

c

SALESPERSON

An eco-friendly fabric garment wholesale company is seeking an energetic self-motivated salesperson (who / whom) likes to travel and drive long distances.

Textile experience preferred (and / but) not essential.

Part-time or full-time vacancy available (and / that) hours flexible.

Please send resume to:

gofortittextiles.com.au

d

MAKE MONEY FROM LETTERBOXES

Local distributors need reliable young people (whom / who) like to earn easy extra cash to deliver newspapers and catalogues in your area.

No experience necessary (and / but) you must be available at short notice (as / and) be able to deliver on time.

Get paid (but / and) get fit walking in your friendly neighbourhood, delivering our quality newspapers and catalogues.

Call Omar 0400 698 872

Name: Due date: Guardian signature:

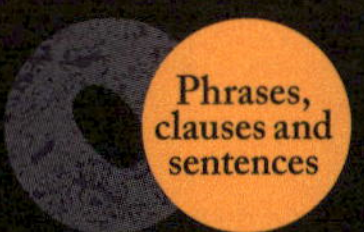

REVISION TEST 5

1 Each of the following passages contains five sentences, but the full stops and capital letters have been left out. Put a cross at the point where each sentence should end. Remember to begin each new sentence with a capital letter.

a Allan Baillie, who emigrated from Scotland with his family when he was a boy, is one of Australia's leading writers for children. many of his stories are survival tales in which children are thrown into dangerous situations the stories are set in many different parts of the world Allan has always been a great traveller and his books are set in countries he has visited one of the most outstanding is *The China Coin*, which is set in China at the time of the massacre in Tiananmen Square

b Libby Gleeson researched her book, *Mahtab's Story*, by talking to Afghan girls who attended Holroyd High School, a school in Sydney's western suburbs the story of the fictitious Mahtab reflects the real experiences of a number of girls whose families had come to Australia as asylum seekers in the novel Mahtab and her family are forced to flee their home in Afghanistan they make a long and dangerous journey across the mountains into Pakistan eventually they manage to make their way from Indonesia to Australia in a very frail boat

c Andy Griffiths is one of Australia's most popular writers for children he also has lots of fans in America on his website he gives some very good advice to people who would like to become published authors he says that it took him 10 years to find a publisher and a writer needs to be stubborn and extremely persistent he also says that it is essential to write every day as you get better at writing by practising constantly

d Joseph Lyons became Australia's prime minister in 1932 he was the first prime minister to win three successive elections and he is still the only Tasmanian to have become prime minister he was nicknamed 'honest Joe' during his prime ministership the Lodge was full of children, as he and his wife Enid had 12 children Enid became the first woman in the House of Representatives and the first woman member of Federal Cabinet

e William (Billy) Hughes became a federal member of parliament in 1901 he became Australia's prime minister in 1915, during the First World War he spent 51 years in the House of Representatives, making him the longest-serving Australian parliamentarian he helped found three political parties and was expelled from them all one of them was the Labor Party, which he helped found in 1916

f Edmund Barton was Australia's first prime minister, taking up office on 1 January 1901 he had a background in law in Australia's first parliament he also held the External Affairs portfolio after leaving politics he worked for 17 years as a High Court Judge he was the second Australian to receive a knighthood

2 Underline the embedded clauses in the following sentences.

a *The Watch that Ends the Night*, which was published in 2011, is about the sinking of the *Titanic*.

b Allan Wolf, who wrote the book, did a huge amount of research into the lives of the passengers and crew who were aboard the ship.

c He tells the story, which is very moving, in the voices of some of those passengers and crew.

d John Snow, who was an undertaker in Halifax, Nova Scotia, tells of the traumatic search for bodies.

e Jamila, who is a refugee from Lebanon, is a teenage girl who is travelling with her younger brother, Elias.

f Jamila and Elias, who survive the shipwreck, have had to leave their father behind, as he did not pass the medical inspection.

3 Decide what difference the commas make to the meaning of these sentences.

a Underline the sentence that implies that all teenagers are noisy.

i Teenagers, who are very noisy, will be asked to leave.

ii Teenagers who are very noisy will be asked to leave.

b Underline the sentence that implies that all head chefs can be hard to work for.

i Head chefs who are very temperamental can be hard to work for.

ii Head chefs, who are very temperamental, can be hard to work for.

c Underline the sentence that implies that all teachers work too hard.

i Teachers, who work too hard, can become quite stressed.

ii Teachers who work too hard can become quite stressed.

d Underline the sentence that implies that all sports celebrities behave badly.

i Sports celebrities who behave badly in public are poor role models.

ii Sports celebrities, who behave badly in public, are poor role models.

e Underline the sentence that implies that all politicians are undervalued.

i Politicians, who are driven by a desire to serve the public, are undervalued.

ii Politicians who are driven by a desire to serve the public are undervalued.

Name: | Due date: | Guardian signature:

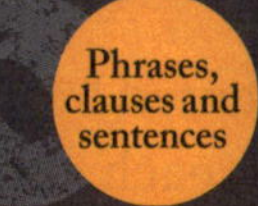

SPELLING FOCUS 2

English spelling is difficult. English speakers have happily borrowed words from other languages through contact with different cultures. We have either continued to spell the word the way it was spelt in the borrowed language, or we have changed the spelling. For example, the adjective *weirdt*, which is Germanic in origin, was spelt *wyrd* in Old English. Later, in Middle English, the spelling changed to *weird*. We cannot always 'sound out' a word like *weird*, as spelling patterns change through the ages and across regions. You will need to memorise the exceptions to each major spelling rule or convention.

1 One of the areas where English has borrowed very heavily is in the names of food. Here are 15 food words that we use. Complete the correct spelling of the words missing letters.

sa__mon	schnit__ __l	sca__lops
p__ __lla	sauerkr__ __t	zucchi__ __
sak__	fettu__ __ine	spagh__ __ __ __
tof__	sush__	cer__ __l
souvl__ __ __	p__ __za	sou__fle

2 Today, most spelling in the English-speaking world is standard but there is some variation in spelling, particularly between Australian English and American English. Write the Australian English spelling for these American English words in the table below.

American	Australian
judgment	
acknowledgment	
civilize	
usable	
aging	

3 One of the things that makes English spelling tricky is that the same spelling can represent different sounds. In the seven words in column A below, the letter *a* represents six different sounds. Draw a line to match each word in column A with the word in column B that has the same sound.

	Column A	Column B
a	above	car
b	acorn	clap
c	all	mud
d	any	paw
e	last	pet
f	pat	play
g	was	top

4 Just as confusing is the fact that in English spelling the same sound can be represented by different spellings. Read the sentences below. Some words have missing letters. In each case the missing letters make the sound /ar/, as in *far*, but the spelling is different in each word. Rewrite the words, filling in the missing letters. Note: the number of spaces represents the number of letters needed.

a How f__st can you run?

b Are you going to plant those bulbs in the g__ __den?

c The church has an annual baz__ __ __, where lots of second-hand treasures can be found.

d Cut down on saturated fats to ensure a healthy h__ __ __t.

e My __ __nt is my mother's sister.

f His rank in the army is s__ __geant.

g The gal__ __ is a bird native to Australia.

h Put h__ __f the chocolate in the refrigerator for tomorrow.

i Where __ __ __ you going now?

j '__ __! What lovely big eyes you've got,' drooled the wolf.

k There will be a security g__ __ __d at the door to make sure only those with passes are admitted.

l I always eat the chocolate noug__ __ first.

5 In each of the words below, the same four-letter pattern is missing. Can you work out which four letters are missing from each of the words?

a h__ __ __ __t

b w__ __ __ __t

c n__ __ __ __bour

d fr__ __ __ __t

e __ __ __ __teen

f __ __ __ __tieth

g n__ __ __ __

h w__ __ __ __

6 In the list in exercise 5 above, the four-letter pattern sounds the same in all words except one. Which word is the odd one out? Write it on the line below.

____

7 Draw a line to match each *-ough* word in column A with its rhyming word in column B.

	Column A	Column B
a	bough	cow
b	cough	low
c	dough	puff
d	tough	toff

8 In the list of words below, all the missing letters have the same sound, but in each word the spelling is different. Fill in the missing letters. Each space stands for one missing letter.

a pl_ _

b cr_che

c matin_ _

d st_ _k

e camp_ _ _n

f gr_ _n

g w_ _ _ _t

h l_te

9 Most – but not all – nouns have a plural form. The majority of nouns in English make their plural by adding *-s*. For example, the plural of *mother* is *mothers*. Some nouns have irregular plurals.

Write the correct plural form for each word in the table below. If you are unsure of a plural form, check the spelling in your dictionary.

	Word	Plural
a	bacterium	
b	balcony	
c	box	
d	butterfly	
e	calf	
f	crisis	
g	criterion	
h	deer	
i	dwarf	
j	fly	
k	foot	
l	gas	
m	half	
n	lash	
o	leaf	
p	life	
q	mouse	
r	oasis	
s	ox	
t	potato	
u	thief	
v	tomato	
w	wolf	

10 Many words in English have silent letters that require correct spelling. Fill in the missing letters in the following words.

a i_land

b resi_n

c b_oyant

d _night

e _reck

f mus_le

g ans_er

h _nee

i lis_ener

j autum_

k _nome

l cu_board

m _nife

n whis_le

o de_tor

11 Silent letters are one of the features that make the spelling of English words tricky. Complete each word below with its missing silent letter. In seven of the words, the silent letter is *k*; in the other three it is *g*.

a _nack

b _nash

c _naw

d _nead

e _nelt

f _night

g _nob

h _nock

i _nome

j _now

12 All the words below are missing the same silent letter. Which letter is it?

a crum_

b thum_

c com_

d de_t

e dum_

f plum_er

g bom_

h dou_t

Name:	Due date:	Guardian signature:

24 PREFIXES AND SUFFIXES

Vocabulary

A **prefix** is a word part that is placed *before* ('pre') other words to change the meaning.

*hyper*active – *hyper* = especially, excessively
*super*natural – *super* = above, beyond
*sub*human – *sub* = less than, under, part of
*re*visit – *re* = again

Many English prefixes have been borrowed from Greek and Latin.

Greek prefixes		
anti	opposite, against	antidepressant, antiseptic, antisocial
para	beside, beyond	paralympics, parallel, parachute
dia	through, across	diagram, diametrical, dialogue
Latin prefixes		
ex	out	exclude, expatriate, exempt
mono	alone, only, single	monologue, monotreme, monotone
trans	across, beyond	transatlantic, transcript, transform

A **suffix** is a letter or group of letters that is added to the end of a root word to form a different word.

dog (root word) add *–s* becomes *dogs* (plural)
read (root word) add *–er* becomes *reader*
beauty (root word) add *–ful* becomes *beautiful*

You will find more about suffixes in Unit 26.

1 Add an appropriate prefix (from the list above) to each keyword below to express the same meaning in one word.

e.g. very sensitive *Answer: hyper*sensitive

a vegetation that has grown again ____________________

b below standard ____________________

c an especially large structure ____________________

d united again ____________________

e extra big or successful star ____________________

f part of the continent ____________________

Knowing the meaning of Latin and Greek prefixes can sometimes help you to work out the meaning of an unfamiliar word.

2 Each of the following words is made up of three parts – a central or root word with a prefix at the beginning and a suffix at the end. Break up each word into its three parts.

e.g. disappearance *Answer*: dis-appear-ance

a immortality ______________________
b unpleasantness ______________________
c disagreement ______________________
d uncertainty ______________________
e unemployment ______________________
f overstatement ______________________
g redevelopment ______________________

TAKE IT FURTHER

1 Provide a word with a prefix for each meaning below.

a vanishing (adjective) ______________________
b cannot be done (adjective) ______________________
c sink below the surface (verb) ______________________
d read incorrectly (verb) ______________________
e be in charge of someone (verb) ______________________

2 Draw a line to match each prefix in the first column to its root word in the second column.

a	auto	bishop
b	hyper	spelling
c	hemi	national
d	bi	cycle
e	inter	tension
f	circum	biography
g	arch	navigate
h	mis	sphere

3 To complete the following sentences choose the correct prefix from the table below.

tele– = distant	*bi–* = two
trans– = across	*pre–* = before
semi– = half, partly	*micro–* = very small, minute

a The ________scope at Parkes is enormous.
b The commentators gave a long ________view of the game.
c You must check every credit card ________action.
d The newly appointed School Captain paused before she spoke into the ________phone.
e I think I need ________focal spectacles to help me read.
f The ________trailer was parked illegally.

Name: Due date: Guardian signature:

25 NEGATIVE PREFIXES

Vocabulary

A **prefix** is a word part placed before a root word to create a new word. Negative prefixes change the meaning of a word to its opposite.

e.g.

non-appearance	*un*natural
*mis*understand	*dis*unity
*de*regulate	*anti*social

Some prefixes are followed by a hyphen to prevent misreading. Check your dictionary if you are unsure about when to add a hyphen.

1 Write the missing negative prefix in the sentences below. Choose from: *de–*, *dis–*, *non–*, *un–* or *mis–*. You will need to add a hyphen to one example.

- **a** She didn't check the points before handing her score to the judge. That is so ______professional.
- **b** They had a huge ______agreement and now they're not talking to each other.
- **c** The priest at our church said it was ______ethical not to support the homeless.
- **d** I had an odd job yesterday; I had to ______frost the freezer.
- **e** Fatima didn't enjoy reading the book because there were so many ______prints in it.
- **f** The soldier stood shaking after he successfully ______fused the bomb.
- **g** He plays football for fun, so he is a ______professional.
- **h** Our neighbour's dog is very ______obedient. It rarely comes when it's called.
- **i** You ______understood what I said.
- **j** Your work is quite ______satisfactory.

TAKE IT FURTHER

1 Work in a pair to find three words for each of the following prefixes. Use a dictionary or thesaurus if you need to.

- **a** non– ______________________________
- **b** de– ______________________________
- **c** dis– ______________________________
- **d** anti– ______________________________
- **e** mis– ______________________________
- **f** in– ______________________________
- **g** un– ______________________________
- **h** im– ______________________________

Check whether a double letter is needed when you add a prefix to a word.

2 Underline the antonym in each set of adjectives below.

e.g. careful, cautious, reckless, prudent

- **a** large, massive, immense, tiny
- **b** poor, rich, wealthy, affluent
- **c** modern, contemporary, old-fashioned, new
- **d** busy, energetic, lazy, industrious
- **e** good-natured, angry, infuriated, irate
- **f** dangerous, secure, hazardous, risky
- **g** cheerful, sullen, uncooperative, unhelpful
- **h** unimaginative, creative, inventive, original
- **i** courageous, brave, cowardly, valiant

1 Look at the word in capital letters on each line below. From the four words following it, underline the synonym – the one that has almost the same meaning.

e.g. SMALL – size, big, little, tall

- **a** WEIGHTY – light, heavy, kilogram, measurement
- **b** TIRED – bored, weary, exhaustion, tiring
- **c** WEALTHY – rich, generous, well-meaning, healthy
- **d** CHEAP – dear, inexpensive, cheerful, miserable
- **e** ROUGH – tough, gentle, tactile, coarse
- **f** WEAK – strong, tired, little, feeble
- **g** POWERFUL – mighty, proud, severe, political
- **h** SLEEK – satin, smooth, smoothness, rough
- **i** STURDY – strength, muscular, strong, fitness
- **j** ANCIENT – ancestor, old, age, youthful

2 Draw a line to match each word in the first column with its antonym in the second column.

a	affluent	inaudible
b	proud	dull
c	audible	destitute
d	cowardly	clumsy
e	bright	lazy
f	merciful	discouraging
g	encouraging	smelly
h	agile	humble
i	fragrant	heroic
j	diligent	merciless

Name: | Due date: | Guardian signature:

28 INCLUSIVE LANGUAGE

Vocabulary

People have come to recognise that some common nouns discriminate against women when the nouns are used in certain contexts. The common noun *man* is an example:

e.g. Since ancient times, *man* has enjoyed sharing food with others.

The writer means people in general, not just male human beings, so we should replace *man* with *humanity* (singular noun) or *people* (plural noun):

e.g. Since ancient times, *people* have enjoyed sharing food with others.

Sexism is discrimination on the basis of gender (female or male), so **gender-specific nouns**, such as *businessmen* rather than *business people*, are naming words that give a discriminatory or stereotyped view of people's jobs or positions of responsibility. Language that is gender-specific is discriminatory and should be avoided.

1 Write a non-sexist word to replace each gender-specific term in the following list.

	Gender-specific	Non-sexist
a	actress	
b	air hostess	
c	airman	
d	batsman	
e	cameraman	
f	cleaning lady	
g	craftsman	
h	crewman	
i	foreman	
j	layman	
k	male nurse	
l	mankind	
m	manpower	
n	policeman	
o	salesman	
p	sportsman	
q	workman	

The third-person singular personal pronouns in English (*he*, *she*) are **gender-specific**. In the past, assumptions were made about the gender of people in certain jobs or professions.

e.g. A doctor needs a good relationship with *his* patients.
A nurse needs a good relationship with *her* patients.

This is **stereotyping** and it no longer reflects the real world. However, there is no gender-neutral pronoun in English so avoiding stereotyping can lead to awkward sentences.

e.g. A doctor needs a good relationship with *his or her* patients.

In speech, we often solve the problem by using *they*, *them* and *their* as substitutes.

e.g. A doctor needs a good relationship with *their* patients.

The use of a plural pronoun (*their*) with a singular noun is not grammatically correct, but it has become very common in cases like this and is now acceptable except in very formal writing. However, you can usually rephrase the sentence. One way of solving the problem is by making the whole sentence plural.

e.g. *Doctors* need a good relationship with *their* patients.
If students have poor study habits, they should seek advice and assistance.

Note that you may not need *their* if you have an adjective before the noun.

e.g. Doctors need a good relationship with *all (their)* patients.

You can also rewrite the sentence using the pronoun *you*.

e.g. If you have poor study habits, you should seek advice and assistance.

1 Change the following gender-specific sentences by using either third-person plural pronouns (*they/them*) or the second person pronoun (*you*).

a A doctor does his best to help patients.

b A truck driver enjoys a good laugh during his break.

c Does a secretary receive appreciation for her work?

d A kindergarten teacher needs to be friendly but firm with her students.

e A barrister spends most of his day in court.

f A good bus driver will help his elderly passengers on board.

g A nurse should provide comfort and care for her patients.

Name: | Due date: | Guardian signature:

29 MODALITY

Vocabulary

The term 'modality' refers to the choice of words that indicate fine degrees of possibility, probability, certainty or obligation. As you discovered in Unit 6, the most common way of expressing modality is in the choice of modal verbs, such as *can*, *may*, *must* or *should*.

Modality is also conveyed by choosing modal adverbs, such as *possibly*, *probably*, *certainly*; modal adjectives, such as *possible*, *probable*, *certain*; and modal nouns, such as *possibility*, *probability*, *certainty*.

Sometimes modality is expressed without any of these obvious modal words being used. Look at the difference between the following examples:

e.g. Students left the classroom in an orderly fashion.
Students were requested to leave the classroom in an orderly fashion.

In the first sentence, there is no doubt about what happened. How certain is the second sentence?

Look too at the difference between these examples:

e.g. Bone fractures of this kind heal quickly.
In the majority of cases bone fractures of this kind heal quickly.

If you had broken your wrist, which sentence above would you prefer to hear from your doctor?

Being aware of the effect your choice of words can have on the modality of a sentence is very important when you are producing persuasive texts. It is also essential to be aware of how people who want to persuade you of something use modality. Texts that want to persuade or influence you – such as advertisements or speeches that are trying to change your point of view – use high modality to appeal to your emotions. Texts that present a reasoned and objective argument tend to use low modality, allowing for the possibility of different views.

1 Underline the modal words in the following sentences. On the lines after each sentence, write whether the modal word is a *verb*, an *adverb*, an *adjective* or a *noun*.

a Somebody must know something about who committed the crime. ___________

b It is probable that someone knows something about who committed the crime. ___________

c You should always do what makes you happy. ___________

d Charles probably expects to accede to the throne soon. ___________

e Charles possibly expects to accede to the throne soon. ___________

f Maybe I forgot to tell Pierre to meet me at the bus stop. ___________

g A Ferrari is undoubtedly a better car than a Porsche. ___________

h Despite the myths, the probability of a snake bite in Australia is low. ___________

If you are working on a persuasive text, consider your choice of modal words.

2 Rank the sentences below from high to low modality. Write *high*, *medium* or *low* after each sentence.

a i It is clear that you have told me the truth. __________

ii It is likely that you have told me the truth. __________

iii It may be that you have told me the truth. __________

b i You could possibly hand the assignment in next week. __________

ii You can probably hand the assignment in next week. __________

iii You must hand the assignment in next week without fail. __________

c i I insist that you wear your tie to school. __________

ii I suggest that you wear your tie to school. __________

iii I would like you to wear your tie to school. __________

d i I will probably come to the party. __________

ii I will certainly come to the party. __________

iii I will possibly come to the party. __________

e i You must get this finished before the end of the lesson. __________

ii You could get this finished before the end of the lesson. __________

iii You ought to get this finished before the end of the lesson. __________

TAKE IT FURTHER

You are attending a community meeting to discuss a proposed development in the local area. You believe that there should be an environmental assessment before the local council makes a decision on the development.

After each sentence write whether it is *high*, *medium* or *low* modality.

a i An environmental assessment is the only appropriate option for this project. __________

ii An environmental assessment is the most desirable option for this project. __________

iii An environmental assessment is one option to be considered for this project. __________

b i It seems likely that native frogs could be threatened by the development. __________

ii Native frogs will be threatened by the development. __________

iii Native frogs may be threatened by the development. __________

c i That's nonsense. You should have checked your facts. __________

ii That's open to question. I suggest that you might check your facts. __________

iii That's an interesting perspective. It may be that some fact checking will reveal other possible positions on the matter. __________

Name:	Due date:	Guardian signature:

30 CHANGES IN THE ENGLISH LANGUAGE OVER TIME

Vocabulary

Languages change all the time. The English language has changed more than most because of its long history of contact with people speaking other languages.

In the 5th century, the **Angles, Saxons and Jutes** began invading England. The tribes who had lived in the area for some thousand years – the Celts – were mostly driven out to the north and west. Their ancestors are the people of Wales, Scotland and Ireland, and their Celtic languages are very different from English.

The invading tribes spoke closely related languages and, over the centuries, they developed a common spoken language, which we now know as **Old English**. Old English is quite different from the English we use today. To a modern reader it looks like a foreign language, although many of the words we use most frequently come from Old English. However, the way we organised those words – the grammar of the language – is rather different. The relationships between words – which word was the subject and which was the object, for example – were shown by the use of an ending on the word, as in languages such as Latin.

A new wave of invaders arrived in England from 747 CE onwards. Over the next 200 years, many **Vikings** settled, especially in the north of England. They spoke a Germanic language and had numerous words in common with the languages of the Angles, Saxons and Jutes, but it seems that there was some confusion with word endings. By the time of the **Norman Conquest** of 1066 – the single biggest event in the history of the English language – Old English was becoming less reliant on word endings and more reliant on the subject–verb–object word order that is the norm in modern English.

When the Normans invaded, England became a country of two languages. The invaders spoke Norman French; their subjects spoke English, which was for a long time regarded as a far inferior language. The two groups had to communicate and, over a period of a few hundred years, the extraordinary result was that, by the middle of the 14th century, English was the official language of England. The language of the conquered had won out over the language of the conquerors. The language that emerged is called **Middle English**.

The second biggest influence on the history of the English language was the period that began with the age of adventure. This is the period known as **Early Modern English**. As the British began to explore the world, they absorbed the huge impact of the Greek, Latin and Renaissance influences on the English vocabulary.

As the British explorers and then empire-builders travelled, the English language not only spread to other parts of the world, it also acquired thousands of words from other languages. One of the distinctive features of the English language has been this ability to absorb words from elsewhere.

This ability to absorb new words and to invent new words from existing resources is alive and well in 21st-century English. Language change has been especially rapid to cope with advances in technology.

1 Google a map of the United Kingdom and identify Wales, Scotland and Ireland – the areas to which the original inhabitants, the Celts, fled when the Angles, Saxons and Jutes invaded and settled in England.

All living languages change over time.

2 Old English did not make nouns plural by adding an *-s* – that was something that was introduced by the French after the Norman Conquest. Look at the following words, which still make their plurals the way they were made in Old English. Talk with a partner and explain how the plurals were made. (Hint: there are two different ways of making words plural in the examples below.)

Singular	Plural
man	men
woman	women
goose	geese
foot	feet
tooth	teeth

Singular	Plural
mouse	mice
louse	lice
child	children
person	people
ox	oxen

3 The fact that English and French were both spoken in England for some hundreds of years after the Norman Conquest led to some interesting pairs of words. The novelist Sir Walter Scott was the first to notice the following pairs.

Old English	Norman French
sheep	mutton
ox	beef
calf	veal

Old English	Norman French
pig	pork
deer	venison
hen	poultry

Can you explain the difference between the two lists? (Hint: think about what were probably the different jobs of the English peasants and the more privileged Norman French household servants.)

Here is the beginning of the Lord's Prayer at different times in the history of the English language. Discuss the differences with a partner.

Old English

Fæder ure þu þe eart on heofonum; Si þin nama gehalgod

Middle English

Oure fadir that art in heuenes, halewid be thi name

Early Modern English

Our Father which art in heaven, hallowed be thy name

Modern English

Our Father in heaven, hallowed be your name

Name: Due date: Guardian signature:

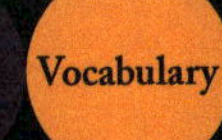

REVISION TEST 6

Vocabulary

1 Fill in the antonyms of the words in the following table, forming the opposites by adding a prefix. Choose from *un–*, *dis–*, *il–*, *im–*, *in–* or *ir–*.

a	regular	
b	honest	
c	legal	
d	mortal	
e	likely	
f	adequate	
g	sane	
h	polite	
i	flexible	
j	mobile	
k	possible	
l	active	
m	definite	
n	secure	
o	probable	
p	expensive	
q	obedient	
r	equal	
s	inhabited	
t	bearable	

2 Sort these 20 adjectives into five groups, each one containing four synonyms. You may not know all the words, but by a process of elimination you should be able to work them out.

abhorrent	fiery	massive	cranky	imperative
fervent	loathsome	commanding	impassioned	weighty
irritable	bulky	heavy	revolting	dictatorial
ardent	hateful	peremptory	crotchety	irascible

a Group 1: ______

b Group 2: ______

c Group 3: ______

d Group 4: ______

e Group 5: ______

3 Form an abstract noun from each word below by adding one of the suffixes from the list.

–ship	–ness	–ice	–dom
–age	–hood	–ism	

a coward ____________

b king ____________

c ideal ____________

d hero ____________

e shrink ____________

f child ____________

g just ____________

h patriot ____________

i bond ____________

j free ____________

k sudden ____________

l bitter ____________

4 Circle the gender-specific noun then rewrite it and the sentence in the plural.

a A doctor is widely respected in his community.

____

b A truck driver likes to buy himself a hearty breakfast of bacon and eggs.

____

c Does a nurse receive appreciation for her work?

____

d A kindergarten teacher is skilled in stimulating a child's imagination and she looks after his physical needs.

____

____

5 Write whether the following sentences are *high*, *medium* or *low* modality.

a You must bring cans of food tomorrow for the charity drive. ____________

b Perhaps you should not wear pink. ____________

c It is likely that you will fail if you don't work harder. ____________

d Checkout closed. ____________

Name:	Due date:	Guardian signature:

31 PUNCTUATING SENTENCE ENDINGS

Punctuation

A sentence is a group of words including a finite verb that makes sense on its own. Most sentences are statements and end with a **full stop**.

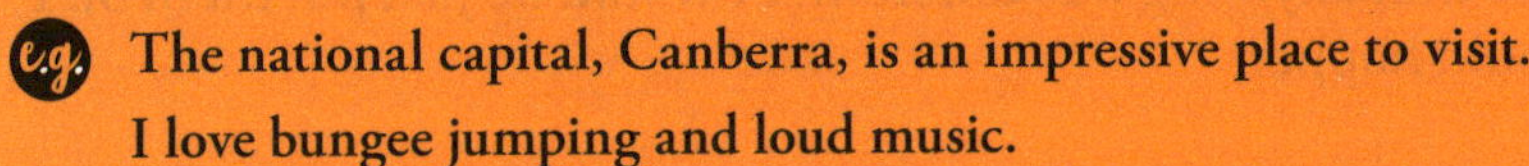

e.g. The national capital, Canberra, is an impressive place to visit.

I love bungee jumping and loud music.

A **question mark** is used in place of a full stop to show that the sentence is a question.

e.g. Did he?

When do you want to go to the shops?

Some sentences are commands or exclamations. Many of these end with a full stop but sometimes we use an **exclamation mark** to express strong feeling. There is no rule about when an exclamation mark is needed. You must decide on the appropriateness in each case. However, exclamation marks should be used sparingly.

e.g. Read silently to concentrate on the story.

Stop, thief!

1 Add a full stop, a question mark or an exclamation mark at the end of each sentence below.

- **a** My stepfather dropped me off at school today ___
- **b** Chop off her head ___
- **c** Do you think this colour suits me ___
- **d** Sit down, now ___
- **e** The dog always yelps with joy when she sees us ___
- **f** Mum, what are we doing today ___
- **g** May I help you ___
- **h** Get out ___
- **i** Why are you carrying that suitcase ___
- **j** Please read from page 162 of your textbooks ___
- **k** Hello, is this David ___
- **l** That's not the way ___
- **m** I have a present for you ___

Don't overdo exclamation marks. They are like using capitals in emails – YOU DON'T WANT TO SHOUT AT YOUR READERS.

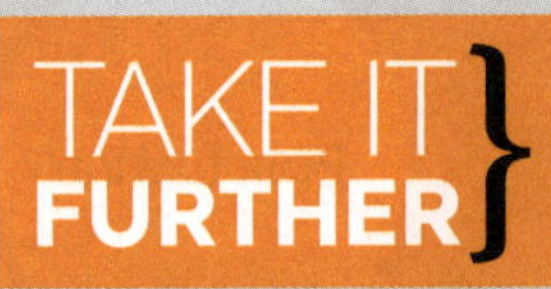

1 Rewrite the following two paragraphs with full stops and question marks. Don't forget to add a capital letter at the beginning of a sentence.

a The label said it was made from the juice of grubs it was guaranteed to create pockmarks it was just what I wanted I rubbed the stuff in his shorts and then I made sure they were neatly folded would he notice that anything was different, or would he just put them on I couldn't wait to see what would happen

b The princess bent down did she know what she was doing she wasn't sure it was a long way down she kissed the little toad on his greasy snout the kiss was sensational it made him grow and change she could not believe her eyes he grew into an old man

2 Rewrite the following student email using full stops, question marks or exclamation marks where they are needed.

Don't embarrass me ever again in front of my friends, Peter why did you do that yesterday in class it's really cut me you could at least apologise when are you going to Mandy reckons I deserve much much better I'm sick of it I try to be good to you and the gang and I get this stuff get it hello I just don't understand guys like you

Name: | Due date: | Guardian signature:

32 COMMAS

Punctuation

Commas are used to show a brief pause in a sentence to make the meaning clear to the reader. They have several precise functions.

→ They are used to separate items in a list.

e.g. **My sister enjoys playing netball, tennis, softball and basketball.**

→ They can be used to separate non-essential information in a sentence.

e.g. **Ms Kouros, the new teacher, is interested in astronomy.**
Dave Warner, who lives in Sydney, is a great cricketer.

However, a comma should not be used when you are expressing a simple statement.

e.g. **My cousin Dave is a brilliant computer analyst. (shows which of my cousins)**
The English explorer Captain Cook was born in Yorkshire. (shows which English explorer)

→ Commas are also used in direct speech before the closing quotation mark (see Unit 37) and to indicate the person being addressed.

e.g. **'Remember to return your library book today,' her mother called.**
'Huang, please call again.' (indicates a person spoken to)

1 Punctuate the sentences below with commas to show the list of items in each.

a The hiker carefully checked her backpack for a water bottle jacket snack compass and map.

b The student dreamed about his holidays of sun swimming surfing sleep-ins and no homework.

c To make this stir-fry you will need beef strips rice noodles mixed vegetables roasted peanuts and chilli jam.

d For the examination you will need writing paper pens and pencils a rubber a pencil sharpener a ruler and a calculator.

2 Punctuate the sentences below with commas to separate non-essential information.

a Smoking a dirty habit is prohibited in public buildings.

b The elderly man who was sitting down looked as if he had had a terrible fright.

c Shaun Tan the author of *The Arrival* is a highly original artist.

d Brisbane the capital of Queensland is a vibrant and sophisticated city.

3 Punctuate the direct speech in the sentences below with commas.

a She called back to her friend 'Thanks for playing today.'

b 'Nicodemus come into my cave ' invited the hermit.

c 'Can you cut up these onions ' Mum asked 'and then fry them in a little butter?'

The most common error with commas is using a comma where you really need a full stop to end a sentence.

1 Insert commas where appropriate in the sentences below.

- **a** Mr Umble peered into a big murky weird bowl full of soft shimmering salty sea-green water.
- **b** A small jellyfish at the bottom of the bowl was moving here there and everywhere.
- **c** 'I don't think I'll go for a bike ride after all' said Mandy.
- **d** The teacher shouted 'And make sure those assignments are on my desk in the morning.'
- **e** I stopped in my tracks when I saw what was on the road in front of me but there was nothing for it I had to pass it somehow.
- **f** 'You're mistaken if you think I'll let you stay up to watch that movie tonight' said Jackie's mum.
- **g** 'I would like one ham and cheese one tomato and one salad sandwich please' requested the hungry boy.
- **h** Even though Tariq had asked his parents not to watch his performance they had secretly bought tickets.

2 The commas are missing in the following Year 7 English subject report. Rewrite it, adding commas where they are needed. You will need seven commas.

> Ejur's results are commendable this semester. Her work on writing folio novel study wide reading and composition showed her consistent enthusiastic approach. She particularly enjoyed poetry appreciation play readings and the oral task. Ejur who is new to this school will gradually develop more confidence volunteering her comments more often in class discussion.

Name:	Due date:	Guardian signature:

33 APOSTROPHES FOR CONTRACTIONS

Punctuation

The **apostrophe** can be used to indicate that one or more letters have been left out of a word.

e.g. *It's* wise to try your best in all endeavours. (*It's* = *It is*)
You're well prepared for the test. (*You're* = *You are*)

1 Complete the table according to the instructions.

Write the contracted form		Write out the contractions in full	
it is		won't	
does not		didn't	
they are		couldn't	
were not		she'll	
you are		I'd	
cannot		he's	
I will		aren't	
let us		there's	
we have		isn't	
I am		could've	

2 Some common spelling errors in English involve confusion between a word that needs an apostrophe for contraction and a word with a different meaning and spelling but the same sound: *it's* is confused with *its*, *you're* with *your*, *they're* with *their* or *there*, and *who's* with *whose*.

Write the following contractions in full:

a it's ____________________

b you're ____________________

c they're ____________________

d who's ____________________

3 Underline the correct choice for each of the following sentences.

a (They're / Their) coming to the party tonight.

b The cat was licking (its / it's) paw.

c (You're / Your) no friend of mine.

d (Its / It's) good to be home.

e Can you give me (they're / their) number?

f Which is (you're / your) favourite?

Misspelling little words can give a bad impression. These are easy if you check them: *it's*, *its*; *you're*, *your*; *they're*, *their* or *there*; *who's*, *whose*.

e The items we were told to bring were eggs, milk, bread, butter and coffee.

f On the stationery list for next year there is a USB drive, a box of blank DVDs and the usual binders.

2 Punctuate the following sentences correctly with semicolons.

a The offender knew the game was up he could see them all waiting for him to come out.

b The siren has sounded it's time for the game to begin.

c The truant stood outside the office for a long time someone told him to wait there.

d I don't like your tone of voice your attitude is offensive.

TAKE IT FURTHER

Punctuate the following sentences using a colon or semicolon.

a Here is the list of what I bought at the school canteen salad rolls, fruit and mineral water.
b As my English teacher once said 'Reading should be a pleasure.'
c The coach appointed Elektra as captain she is the best player.
d Hamlet said 'To be, or not to be.'
e I was carrying too much maths books, sports gear, lunch and folders.
f I was worrying far too much I was grateful when Li offered to help.

Name: | Due date: | Guardian signature:

36 PUNCTUATING TITLES

Punctuation

Capitals are required for the titles of books, songs, films, television and stage shows, plays, poems, brand names, restaurants and ships. Capitals are not needed in a multiword title for less important words, such as *the*, *and*, *of*, *in* or *a*, unless these words come at the beginning of the title.

Harry Potter and the Philosopher's Stone
Advance Australia Fair
Ashiana
Singing in the Rain
The One Day of the Year

1 Rewrite the following titles with capitals.

a world news Australia ______________________

b a current affair ______________________

c curse of the cat people ______________________

d king of thieves ______________________

Titles of books, newspapers, magazines, films, television programs and plays are underlined in handwriting and italicised in printed text.

e.g. Morris Gleitzman's *Once* is both very, very funny and terribly sad, often both at the same time. Every chapter in *Once* begins with 'Once upon a time'.

The names of ships are also either italicised or underlined.

e.g. The *QE2*, on its last voyage, passed the new liner, the *Queen Victoria*, in Sydney Harbour.

2 Rewrite the following sentences, using capitals and underlining for italics where necessary.

a the fellowship of the ring is a better film than spectre.

b to kill a mockingbird is one of the best books I have read.

c the hmas sydney sailed alongside the uss truman in the pacific ocean.

d After we saw matilda, we went to dinner at this great chinese restaurant called oriental star.

Italics are represented in handwriting by underlining.

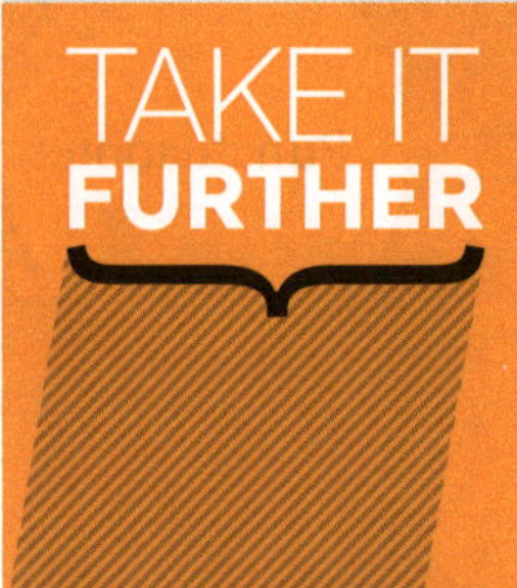

While titles of books, films, television series and so on are italicised (or underlined in handwriting), parts within those works are punctuated with quotation marks. This includes episodes in a television series, and individual stories, essays or poems within a collection.

My favourite poem in Steven Herrick's book *Naked Bunyip Dancing* is 'Billy's Surprise'.

My favourite episode in the teen television series *Dance Academy* is 'The Audition'.

1 Punctuate the following sentences correctly. (Use underlining to indicate italics.)

a henry lawson's famous story of outback hardship, the drover's wife, was first published in his book when the billy boils.

b you will find a copy of henry lawson's poem the ballad of the drover in the anthology the power of poetry.

c my favourite scene in mad max: fury road is where max rockatansky fights immortan joe.

d In shakespeare's play hamlet, hamlet is deeply depressed by his father's death and his mother's hasty re-marriage.

e In the action film the martian, the role of astronaut mark watney is played by matt damon.

f In the comedy a midsummer night's dream by william shakespeare, puck is a funny character.

Name: | Due date: | Guardian signature:

37 PUNCTUATING DIRECT SPEECH

Punctuation

Direct speech or **real speech** refers to the words actually spoken by a person. Quotation marks (“ ” or ‘ ’) are used to show direct speech and are used in pairs. A capital letter is needed for the first word inside the quotation marks. You must start a new line for a change of speaker.

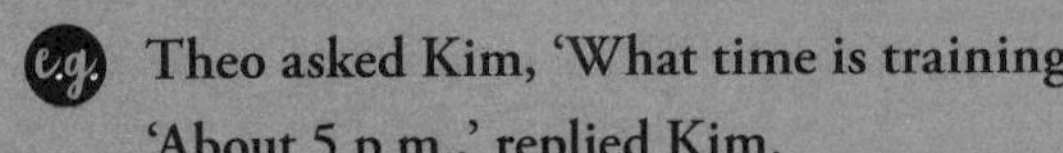

e.g. Theo asked Kim, ‘What time is training?’
‘About 5 p.m.,’ replied Kim.

Most writers like to use single quotation marks (‘ ’) rather than double quotation marks (“ ”) because they are simpler to key on a computer. Either is acceptable. When quotation marks are needed within a quotation, use both ‘ ’ and “ ”.

e.g. ‘Will you sing “Wonderwall” to end the concert?’ asked the promoter.
‘The ending of that story “The Pied Piper of Hamelin” is just horrible!’ cried the boy.

When a quotation has its own punctuation mark – such as a full stop, a question mark or an exclamation mark – it is placed within the quotation marks.

e.g. ‘Did you see that?’ screamed the commentator. ‘The goalie simply missed the ball!’

Quotation marks are also called speech marks or inverted commas.

1 Add quotation marks to the following sentences.

- **a** What on earth do you think you’re doing? yelled my father.
- **b** Patrick said, If you don’t give me the bat immediately, I’ll tell the teacher.
- **c** Turn that music down! said her mother.
- **d** I think, said the professor, that we ought to take a little visit to your cave in the forest.
- **e** I think I’d rather clean up the litter than go on detention, Shelley whispered to her friend.
- **f** It seemed like forever, but finally Mum sighed and said, Oh, I suppose so.
- **g** Come on, encouraged her friend. It’s not far from here.
- **h** Sharif, would you like to go to a movie with me? Emilio asked.
- **i** I really like the excitement and skill level of the World Cup teams, said Imran.

2 In the following sentences, shade the balloons where you think a quotation mark should be.

- **a** What’s your favourite film, Tom? the teacher asked.
- **b** I love the *Harry Potter* series, Tom replied.
- **c** My favourite, he said, is the last one in the series.

Start a new line for each new speaker when writing dialogue.

1 Rewrite the following text with appropriate quotation marks for direct speech. Remember to use a new line for each change of speaker.

Who is the prettiest of them all? You are, sweetie, for a while, replied the mirror. What do you mean? shouted the queen. That pretty Cinderella can't wait to get her little feet into this big palace, replied the mirror. My foot, she will! cried the queen.

2 In the pairs of sentences below, one sentence is in direct speech and requires quotation marks. The other is in indirect or reported speech – a summary of what the speaker said. You will notice that changes in person and tense occur when indirect or reported speech is used. Pick out the direct speech and rewrite the sentence, putting in the quotation marks where they are needed. You might also need a capital letter in some cases.

a i What's your favourite book? he asked.

ii He asked me what was my favourite book.

b i *The Incredible Adventures of Cinnamon Girl*, I replied.

ii I replied that it was *The Incredible Adventures of Cinnamon Girl*.

c i He wanted to know why that was my favourite.

ii Why's that your favourite? he wanted to know.

d i I explained that it was because it was both sad and funny at the same time.

ii I explained, because it's both sad and funny at the same time.

e i He asked, have you seen the play that is based on the book?

ii He asked if I had seen the play that is based on the book.

Name: Due date: Guardian signature:

REVISION TEST 7

1 Rewrite the following extract, putting in all the necessary punctuation. You will need to begin a new paragraph at some points.

when i flicked the light on mum nearly dropped her bags billy youre filthy youve been fighting at school again dad said me i replied innocently i dont fight kids pick on me dad you know that you must do something to provoke them mum said mind your own business and theyll mind theirs it worked for me dad added

______

______

______

______

______

2 Rewrite the following recipe, putting in all the necessary punctuation.

melt 50 g butter in a heavy frying pan over medium heat and fry one thinly sliced onion until soft add 2 tablespoons of paprika and cook for a couple of minutes being careful not to let the onion burn add 300 g of halved button mushrooms and cook for a further five minutes remove from the pan add one tablespoon of oil to the pan and cook 800 g of beef strips in batches return mushroom and onion mix to pan pour in 300 mL of light cream bring to the boil and simmer for one minute stir in the juice of half a lemon and sprinkle with chopped parsley

______

______

______

______

______

______

______

3 Pick out the sentences where an apostrophe has been left out. Write out the word where the apostrophe is needed, putting the apostrophe in the correct place. Not all sentences need an apostrophe.

a Every childs bag must be labelled. ______

b The cars bumper has been damaged in the collision. ______

c The library books are to be returned tomorrow. ______

d The books cover is torn. ______

9780170389501

e The cars were queued by the tollgate. ______________________________

f The guinea pigs cage needs cleaning. ______________________________

g The dogs grabbed the boys cap. ______________________________

h Childrens toys must be stowed safely. ______________________________

4 Each sentence below is missing one comma. Write down the word that should be followed by a comma.

a I ordered bacon eggs and tomato for breakfast. __________

b The table next to me ordered kebabs tacos and burritos. __________

c Orange juice cereals and toast were available on a side table. __________

d You could also order tea coffee or hot chocolate. __________

5 Underline the sentence that means that accommodation is not available to any teenagers.

a I will not let rooms to teenagers who play loud music all night.

b I will not let rooms to teenagers, who play loud music all night.

6 Underline the sentence that means that Paul is keen on Janet.

a Janet thinks Paul is gorgeous.

b Janet, thinks Paul, is gorgeous.

7 Punctuate the following sentences using a colon or semicolon.

a This is my brother's Christmas list a guitar, PlayStation and some pairs of jeans.

b The principal made the following announcement 'Sport will be cancelled today because of the bad weather.'

c Tanya is to play the lead in the school play she is by far the best actor.

d Polonius said to his son, who was leaving to go to university 'Neither a borrower nor a lender be.'

e Polonius sounds like a mean old man I would hope that my friends would lend things to me if I needed them.

f Just last week I borrowed the following from my best mate his answers to the maths homework, his PE gear because I'd left mine at home and some lunch money because I'd forgotten to bring any.

Name:	Due date:	Guardian signature:

Punctuation

SPELLING FOCUS 3

English has a huge number of homophones – words that sound the same but have different spellings and meanings. Mostly they are pairs of words, but there are a few groups of four or five words that sound the same. Some homophones are the most commonly misspelt words in the language, especially little words such as *it's* and *its*, *your* and *you're*, *who's* and *whose*, and *there*, *they're* and *their*.

One reason why these are so tricky is that computer spellcheck programs can't tell which homophone you should be using in a sentence. You simply have to learn them.

1 Underline the correct homophone in each bracketed pair below.

a The (sum / some) was too difficult for the student to calculate.

b (Sum / Some) people seem to have all the fun.

c The boy was not (hear / here) when the awards were presented.

d Anil did not (hear / here) when his mother called.

e (Nun / None) of the survivors suffered trauma afterwards.

f The (nun / none) prayed in the chapel.

g I ate a (pair / pare / pear) for lunch.

h I bought a (pair / pare / pear) of shoes.

i I want to (pair / pare / pear) the overhanging bush with clippers.

j How can you (bear / bare) that loud music?

k Do not (bear / bare) too much skin when you are in the sun.

l Our new (principal / principle) likes to talk about developing students' literacy as well as their aspirations and talents.

m I don't know (whether / weather) I'll do a digital illustration or try my hand at a sketch.

2 Here are some commonly confused pairs of homophones. Find the right one in each sentence.

a stationery – stationary

i The traffic had been ______________ for 10 minutes; not one vehicle had moved.

ii You can buy white-out and glue from the ______________ shop.

b aloud – allowed

i Read your story ______________ to the class.

ii You are not ______________ to chew gum in the classroom.

c counsellor – councillor

i The school ______________ can advise you on personal matters.

ii Who will be elected as our local ______________?

d alter – altar

i The bride and groom exchanged vows before the ______________.

ii We have asked the architect to ______________ the plans for the building.

e serial – cereal

Which is your favourite ______________ for breakfast?

f horse – hoarse

I've had a cold and my voice is quite ______________.

g gate – gait

Because he's carrying such a heavy bag, his ______________ is awkward.

h creak – creek

I could hear the door ______________ in the wind.

3 Underline the correct word in each sentence.

a Many businesses will not accept a (check / cheque) for payment.

b The (air / heir) to the throne is the popular prince.

c The (hare / hair) darted at the blast of the shotgun.

d The witness told the (whole / hole) truth in court.

e Your (waist / waste) tells me you eat healthily.

f The (pair / pear) fell off the tree.

4 The most common misspellings in the English language occur in the most common words. Underline the correct spelling in each bracketed pair.

a (Theirs / There's) no doubt that (your / you're) work has improved greatly.

b (Who's / Whose) left this book behind?

c (Who's / Whose) book is this?

d (It's / Its) easy to see that (your / you're) making more effort.

e (There / They're) close friends.

f (They're / Their) coming to the party tonight.

g The cat was licking (its / it's) paw.

h (You're / Your) not easy to persuade.

i (Its / It's) good to be home.

j Can you give me (they're / their) number?

k What's (you're / your) favourite takeaway dinner?

5 Underline the correct words in the following sentence.

(Your / You're) local reporter Zeeta Gdansk enjoys reading books, especially when (it's / its) raining outside, and practising French and Spanish with her pet fish because (their / they're) the only ones that won't laugh at her.

6 American English spelling is sometimes different from Australian and British English spelling. Underline the accepted Australian spelling in each pair of words below.

a offence / offense
b favorite / favourite
c theatre / theater
d woolen / woollen
e donut / doughnut
f traveler / traveller
g centre / center
h skilful / skillful
i honor / honour
j pajamas / pyjamas

7 Here are some American spellings. For each one, write the Australian equivalent.

a flavor ________________
b specter ________________
c pretense ________________
d humor ________________
e caliber ________________
f behavior ________________
g glamor ________________
h marvelous ________________
i jewelry ________________
j modeled ________________
k traveler ________________

8 When a negative prefix is added to a word, sometimes a double letter is needed. Which of the following negative prefixes needs a double letter? Add a second letter in the space if it is needed.

a dis__atisfied
b un__ecessary
c dis__imilar
d il__egal
e un__inhabited
f dis__agree
g il__iterate
h un__oticed
i dis__appoint
j im__ortal
k im__ature
l ir__egular
m ir__esponsible

9 It is important to correctly spell the technical words – called the metalanguage – of each of your subjects. Here are some important words from the metalanguage of English. The words are jumbled. Unjumble them, taking care with the spelling.

a mmaarrg ________________

b mmaoc ________________

c ttnnuuaoicp ________________

d rtsheaoopp ________________

e aehprs ________________

f aeucls ________________

g hhooomenp ________________

h nymosny ________________

i spevais ________________

j joonnnccuit ________________

10 In the words from the metalanguage of English below, insert the missing letters. The number of spaces tells you how many letters are needed.

a gram_atical

b adjectiv_l

c d_scription

d apostro_ _e

e r_ _thm

f rh_me

g play_ _ight

h diction_ry

i auxil_ary

j particip_e

Name: | Due date: | Guardian signature:

38 PARAGRAPHS AND TOPIC SENTENCES

Constructing texts

A **paragraph** is made up of several sentences. A paragraph usually begins with a topic sentence that states the main idea. The sentences that follow in the paragraph relate to the **topic sentence**. Note: sometimes topic sentences are called paragraph openers.

e.g. *Maria is a generous girl.* She volunteered to raise money for the Salvation Army Appeal at her school. Nobody knew she also donated all her savings. Maria is motivated by love for others less fortunate.

→ The idea introduced in the topic sentence is developed in the rest of the paragraph.

→ The details should be relevant and presented in logical order.

→ A well-written paragraph has a clear link with other paragraphs.

1 Read the following run-on text carefully and indicate where it needs to be divided into two paragraphs.

a Love or hate it, sport is a very popular pursuit in Australia. Millions of Australians compete in a huge variety of sports, from football to aerobics. Others prefer just to be spectators so that they can cheer on participants from the stands or their television lounges. Dave Warner is one of the most popular Australian sports stars. He is a fine batsman in the Australian cricket team. We will enjoy watching him make many more runs for Australia as he is one of the best players in the world.

b The solar system is made up of the sun and a variety of celestial bodies that are bound to it by gravity. These bodies include the eight planets and their moons and billions of smaller bodies, such as asteroids and comets. The planet Mars has especially interested human beings throughout history. It is the planet that is nearest to Earth and we have always wondered whether it could sustain life. Observations taken by spacecraft that have landed on Mars suggest that large areas of the planet were once covered by water. However, it is unlikely that little purple creatures with large antennae ever lived there, despite their regular appearance in movies!

c John Flanagan's *Ranger's Apprentice* series has been a huge success. Set in an imaginary Europe that seems to be in the Middle Ages, the novels feature the adventures of young Will and his talented mentor, Halt. Will and Halt have a series of dangerous adventures which they survive because of their exceptional fighting and stealth skills. The novels grew out of a series of stories that John wrote for his 12-year-old son, Michael. Michael, unlike his father at the same age, did not enjoy reading, so John made up stories full of the kind of action and humour that Michael enjoyed.

Every paragraph has a main or topic sentence.

1 Underline the topic sentence in each of the paragraphs below.

> *e.g.* Sport provides mass entertainment on television. Television shows a lot of football and cricket. Sport is a major part of the weekend programs for most commercial stations. Most of the games televised are men's sports.

a Some good used cars cost as little as $3000. Used cars are cheaper to buy now. A few years ago it was almost impossible to buy a reliable car under $6000. It is still important to check the car carefully. It is probably worth having a mechanic look at it before you hand over the cash.

b A trip to the Gold Coast in winter is cheaper. It pays to shop around for bargain holidays. It is easy these days to compare deals on the Internet. Check that prices quoted are fully inclusive.

c Friends are very important. Friends can be both male and female. Good friends will last a lifetime.

d Chocolate was introduced to Europe centuries ago. Cadbury sells a lot of chocolate. Its factory in Hobart has been a popular tourist attraction for many years, but it recently stopped its factory tours. Hygiene requirements are very strict these days.

e At school, students study and do sport. School offers a balanced program for students. Students are also offered programs that allow them to develop their creative talents. A good school has something for everyone.

2 The paragraphs below are missing their topic sentences. Choose the sentence in the list that best fits each paragraph.

- Teenagers have a great sense of humour.
- Sports stars are more popular than politicians.
- Dental care is often neglected.
- Tourism is a major industry in Australia.
- A summer holiday at the beach is better than the hills.

a ________________________________ Some people take the inside of their mouth for granted. They seek treatment only irregularly.

b ________________________________ In such a vast and diverse land there is so much to see. In recent years, there has been an increase of overseas visitors.

c ________________________________ Just ask any teacher or youth worker. Their humour keeps adults on their toes.

d ________________________________ People are more likely to listen to them and look up to them as role models. This seems to be a tradition in Australia unlike some other countries.

e ________________________________ Who wants to hike when you can relax on the sand? You can also see the sunset on the coast.

Name: | Due date: | Guardian signature:

39 COHESIVE TIES WITHIN PARAGRAPHS

Constructing texts

Cohesive ties are words and phrases used by a writer to link or connect phrases, clauses and sentences within paragraphs to convey the meaning.

Phrases, clauses and sentences can be connected by conjunctions, such as *and*, *but* and *or*. See Units 16 and 17.

e.g. The train *and* its passengers were ready for departure.

Clare guessed the answer *but* did not get it right.

Adverbs such as *afterwards*, *next*, *then*, *however* and *consequently* are also used to link sentences. Adverbs used like this are sometimes called connectives. See Unit 14.

e.g. We played volleyball. *Then* we did aerobics in the pool.

She offered to lend me her racquet. *However*, I'd rather use my own.

Text cohesion can also be created by:

→ Pronouns that refer back to nouns, noun groups or clauses

e.g. The fans love *Browny*. *He* is a star footballer.

Abigail told Thomas *she* was going to meet *her* new boyfriend.

She knew *what needed to be done*. *It* would take considerable risk, however.

→ Ellipsis – omitting a word or words that would be clear from the context:

e.g. She knows my father better than me. (Instead of: She knows my father better than *she knows me*.)

I would love to go to Paris, but I can't afford to. (Instead of: but I can't afford to *go to Paris*.)

→ Substitution – replacing a word or phrase with a word that stands for it:

e.g. I have two *bicycles*. My next *one* will be a racer.

Don't *talk* during the test; if you *do*, we'll have to disqualify you.

→ Repetition of words or use of related words, creating a lexical chain of words with similar (or sometimes opposite) meanings. A **lexical chain** is a sequence of related words in writing.

e.g. *Aphrodite* acted in the same school play as you. You do recall *Aphrodite*, don't you?

Wayne and Barry *boxed* to build toughness. *Boxing* is great aerobic exercise too.

Dave replaced the old *TV* with a new *HD Smart LED*.

My speech is about the importance of *liberty* in a democracy. It is easy to take our *freedom* for granted.

1 Recognising whether it is a conjunction or an adverb that is used as a cohesive tie can be tricky. However, it is important. If it is an adverb, you need a full stop and a new sentence. Underline the conjunction or adverb that is used as a connective in the following sentences. In the space, write whether it is an *adverb* or a *conjunction*.

a The team results were very disappointing. Consequently, the class had to come back for extra revision lessons. ____________

b The test results were very disappointing but we expect them to improve next season.

____

Cohesive ties hold paragraphs together.

c The boy lost his computer. However, that was not the only thing he would lose that day. ______________

d The new windscreen wipers were ready to be installed and the brakes had been checked. ______________

e We ran to the faraway tree. Then we climbed to the highest bough. ______________

2 Underline the cohesive tie and name its type (*pronoun, related word, substitution, repetition, ellipsis*) in each of the following sentences.

> *e.g.* Jack and Hilary rowed together. Rowing is the ultimate team sport. *Answer:* Repetition

a I own two pairs of shoes. The next one will be dress boots. ______________

b I don't know anyone who dislikes Wozza. He is the life of the party. ______________

c The young couple saved their money to buy a house. Saving is essential for financial security. ______________

d Dad replaced the old Nissan with a new car. ______________

e Dmitri knows my brother better than me. ______________

f Pam knew the situation would be difficult. It would test her strength of character. ______________

TAKE IT FURTHER

The following short paragraph is clumsy, partly because cohesive ties have not been used. Choose the correct cohesive ties from the list below and write them in the spaces.

(conjunction) and

(adverb) then

(pronoun) he

(substitution) it

I had a wonderful holiday. ______________ was spent at Byron Bay. The first few days were spent surfing with a mate ______________ we went sailing ______________ snorkelling. ______________ couldn't get over the number of colourful underwater fish.

Name: | Due date: | Guardian signature:

40 COHESIVE TIES ACROSS PARAGRAPHS

Constructing texts

Just as cohesive ties are used to give unity or cohesion to the sentences within a paragraph, it is essential that the paragraphs within a text are connected in a way that ensures logical development.

Most of the same cohesive ties that are used to connect sentences within a paragraph are used to connect paragraphs, except for conjunctions. It is unusual (and in most cases incorrect) for conjunctions to link paragraphs. The most common links between paragraphs are adverbs or adverbial phrases such as *afterwards, consequently, however, to begin with* or *in the second place.*

Pronoun referents, ellipses and substitution are also important connectives. However, the most common link between paragraphs is made by lexical chains – words that are related or repeated and words that are synonyms or antonyms.

1 Read the following two paragraphs from a newspaper report. There are some difficult words in the report. Use a dictionary to check their meanings if you are unsure.
Underline the nine words or phrases that form a lexical chain.

> Australia is in the top ten of the richest countries in the world. Our median wealth is US$168,000, which places us third behind affluent Switzerland and New Zealand, and well ahead of the United States, which many of us assume to be very prosperous.
>
> Why, then, do we constantly complain of being poor? Callers to talkback radio say that the cost of living is killing them. Rather than acknowledging that we are well-off, we believe – wrongly – that we are in danger of becoming destitute.

2 Read the following two paragraphs from a blog. Underline the 10 words that form a lexical chain.

> I have set up this blog as a way of sharing my love of food. Cooking has always been my favourite pastime. I have a huge collection of cookery books and I love exploring the cuisine of other countries. Many of my books are by famous chefs from top restaurants around the world.
>
> I would like to share my favourite recipes with readers of my blog. Each blog entry will feature an entrée, a main and a dessert.

Cohesive ties hold whole texts together.

Read the student book report and look for the language features that give the text its cohesion. Draw an arrow from each of the underlined words or phrases to another word or phrase that forms a logical link in the text.

For my book report I have chosen the picture book *Dragon Quest*, written by Allan Baillie and illustrated by Wayne Harris. I have chosen this because I love the way in which the pictures at the end tell a different story to the written words. It's fun to realise that we can see something that one of the characters can't see.

That character is the old Dragon Fighter, who is on a quest to kill the last dragon. As readers, we join the adventure – one that is packed with 'awful perils' and 'dark dangers'. These include crossing a scary desert and a terrifying, haunted forest. Then there is the whispering abyss. It is full of werewolves, demons and dracula bats. Other strange creatures include the two-headed trolls, who cannot be defeated.

These exciting episodes are typical of fantasy quests, where the hero has to overcome one danger after another. As readers we are represented in the pictures by the young boy who joins the old Dragon Fighter as he searches for that last dragon. He is amazed by the boy's suggestion that he has no wish to slay the dragon: it is enough just to see one, especially as it is the last one.

There is a lot of humour in the book, including the fact that we can see the last dragon but the Dragon Fighter can't. I also like the message: you don't have to kill to be 'a hero, a great warrior, an epic knight'.

a In the first paragraph, what does 'something' stand for?

b In the second paragraph, what does 'these' stand for?

c Make a list of the words and phrases that are about fear, making a lexical chain.

d Why is 'another' at the end of paragraph two an example of ellipsis?

e Find an example of ellipsis in the last paragraph and rewrite it here.

f What does 'these exciting episodes' in the third paragraph stand for?

Name: | Due date: | Guardian signature:

REVISION TEST 8

1 Underline the nouns in sentences below. Then write them in the appropriate column in the table.

a Kiki squealed with surprise and delight when the flock of galahs swooped down into the paddock behind the house.

b The congregation listened in awe as the famous choir from Oxford sang the old hymns.

c A battalion of soldiers has been dispatched with great urgency to the flood disaster in Queensland.

Common noun	Proper noun	Abstract noun	Collective noun

2 In each sentence below the same word is used twice: once as a common noun and once as a proper noun. Rewrite the sentences, adding the necessary capitals to the proper nouns.

a He started primary school this year at windsor gardens primary school.

____

b When she goes to a club for dinner, she usually visits the geelong football club.

____

____

c The street where we live leads into cranbrook street.

____

d The most beautiful orchestra I ever heard was the royal philharmonic orchestra.

____

____

e There are several museums worth visiting in canberra, but the one that you must not miss is the national museum of australia.

____

____

f The premiers of all the states held an informal meeting, chaired by the premier of victoria.

____

____

3 Fill in the missing words in the word families table.

	Noun	Verb	Adjective	Adverb
a		satisfy		
b				prosperously
c	reason			
d			laughable	
e			knowledgeable	
f	justice			
g			high	
h		energise		
i				breathlessly
j	clarity			
k				moistly
l	obedience			

4 The word 'fancy' is used in the following three sentences once as an adjective, once as a noun and once as a verb. Write the correct part of speech in the space after each sentence.

a Her room is decorated with fancy cushions. ________________

b I don't fancy your chances. ________________

c I've taken a fancy to that painting. ________________

5 Underline the sentence below that uses the word 'foul' as a noun.

a That's a foul trick.

b You will foul your line if you cast like that.

c He was sent off for a foul.

6 Underline the sentence below that uses the word 'light' as a verb.

a I was dazzled by the bright light.

b When are you going to light the fire?

c I'd prefer that top in a light colour.

7 Underline the phrase(s) in each sentence below.

a We were lying on the lawn.

b Locking the door behind him, Juan hurried towards the garage.

c The table, lavishly decorated, stood in the corner.

8 Each sentence has two main (or coordinate) clauses. Put brackets around each clause and underline the word that joins them.

a My brother loves reading but my sister prefers the outdoors.

b The bicycle swerved dangerously and then it collided with the fence.

c I love food but I don't like cooking.

d The children sang their songs and all the parents applauded.

e He arrived late for the party but he did not apologise.

9 Put brackets around the main clause and underline the subordinate clause in these sentences.

e.g. (My dog is timid) because my cat is so aggressive.

a The balloon escaped into the air while the child watched sadly.

b I want to visit the country where my dad was born.

c When the weather is fine, we go to the beach.

d The black labrador, which is playing with those children, belongs to my brother.

e Juan bought a new iPad, which had lots of extra features.

10 Shade the bubbles to indicate where apostrophes are needed in the following sentences.

a There are plenty of good childrens films to choose from in the stores catalogue.

b Boys who love action will love Toms character in Australias next hit movie.

c Its predicted that its box office sales will beat all previous records.

11 Shade the bubbles to indicate where quotation marks are needed in these sentences.

a I'd love to come to the party, Mary replied, and I'd like to bring Gus.

b My mother shouted, Come on! It's time for dinner!

12 Use prefixes to form the antonyms of the following words.

a respectful ____________

b movable ____________

c audible ____________

d understand ____________

e behave ____________

f dress ____________

g religious ____________

h literacy ____________

i similarity ____________

j obey ____________

13 Punctuate the following conversation, beginning a new line where necessary.

would you like to come to my party mary asked lee you can bring joanne if you like when is it lee replied this saturday at eight oclock mary replied ill check with joanne but im sure that shed like to come lee said I can borrow my brothers car

14 The following sentences are examples of reported or indirect speech. Rewrite them as direct speech, including quotation or speech marks where necessary. You may need to make changes to person and tense.

a Enrico said he wanted to visit Italy to see his grandmother but his soccer tour made it impossible.

b Maria said she found the punctuation homework easy to complete.

c Tan asked Caleb if he would like to come to his place to watch the Grand Final.

d The reporter asked Taylor Swift when her Australian tour would begin.

e The History teacher noted that Anzac Day is often identified with Gallipoli and not so much with the Western Front.

f The Hollywood producer told the reporter that his film has delightful characters.